Holiness: Every Christian's Calling

HOLINESS

Every Christian's Calling

ROGER ROBERTS

BROADMAN PRESS
Nashville, Tennessee

© Copyright 1985 • Broadman Press

All Rights Reserved

4219-56

ISBN: 0-8054-1956-X

Dewey Decimal Classification: 248

Subject Heading: SPIRITUAL LIFE

Library of Congress Catalog Number: 85-11330

Printed in the United States of America

Library of Congress Cataloging in Publication Data

Roberts, Roger, 1945-
  Holiness, every Christian's calling.

  Includes bibliographies.
  1. Holiness. I. Title.
BT767.R56 1985   234'.8   85-11330
ISBN 0-8054-1956-X (pbk.)

To the glory of God,
who calls and enables us to be holy;
With gratitude to my loving wife, Nancy,
and children, Stephanie and Kyle,
for their encouragement in my life and ministry;
And appreciation for the people
of Metropolitan Baptist Church,
Wichita, Kansas, and pastor's secretary, Lesta Foster,
for their support of my preaching and writing.

Contents

Introduction

It is God's will that you should be holy. . . . For God did not call us to be impure, but to live a holy life. 1 Thess. 4:3a; 7

The call came years ago, at the time of my childhood conversion —Not that it was ever totally forgotten. It simply was one of the many callings and demands that occasionally beckoned above the din of a busy life and ministry. But suddenly, amid a personal struggle for my identity and direction as a minister, that call which had never been totally silenced became a welcome word of direction. This voice of God, arising out of my personal Bible study and preaching ministry, reminded me that my primary calling as a Christian is not to perform up to a certain level of ministerial success, either self-imposed or modeled by the many highly-esteemed pastors in the evangelical world. My first and foremost calling, I now understand, *is to be holy.*

Indeed, this primary call was given me before my calling to preach and serve as the pastor of a local congregation. When God, in His infinite grace, chose me to become His child through my faith in Jesus Christ, He also called me to a life of holiness. With this new understanding of my primary call, truths I already knew came into sharper focus and began to expose my identity struggle as little more than the restless stirrings of personal ambition. Unless and until I answered the prior call to be holy, even my best ministerial performance would be tainted by selfish and ambitious

9

motives. Without holiness characterizing my inner life and inter-personal relationships I could not hope to fulfil my responsibilities as a spiritual leader of my congregation, which includes my own family. I began to see that my effectiveness and credibility as a spiritual leader in my home, church, and community hinged upon my willingness to grow in holiness. The call was to strive toward the goal God has for all His children—to be holy and to live a holy life.

This newfound sense of purpose and direction for me begged to be shared with my congregation. While visiting in England I pur-chased a used copy of W. E. Sangster's *The Pure in Heart: A Study of Christian Sanctity,* a scholarly yet inspiring treatise on holiness.[1] The great Methodist preacher, pastor, and denominational leader por-trayed the life of holiness around an exposition of Galatians 5:22-23, the "fruit of the Spirit" passage, giving historic and contempo-rary examples of Christians who took seriously the call to be holy. I preached a series of Sunday night sermons on the subject of holiness, following Sangster's model, and began what I believe should be a lifetime study of this vital subject.

Shortly after entering this study of holiness I realized the vast-ness of the subject. As I searched the Scriptures pertaining to holiness, I realized with new appreciation the pervasiveness of this theme throughout the Bible. A study of the entire Christian life would not be much narrower in scope. The Bible is God's self-revelation and the expression of His will for mankind. And since God is perfectly holy and His will is that His people be holy, then of necessity the Bible is a book about holiness. Not only does a Bible concordance include voluminous scripture references under such words as "holy," "godly," "pure," and "righteous," but also a holistic and thematic study of the Bible portrays the drama

of our great God and Savior, Jesus Christ, who gave himself for us to redeem us from all wickedness and to purify for himself a people that are his very own, eager to do what is good (Titus 2:13-14).

My study has given me a new perspective of the biblical emphasis on holiness, but I also found little has been written in recent years on the subject. A wave of books on the doctrine of the Holy Spirit followed in answer to the neo-Pentecostal movement, but few of these emphasized the believer's calling to the practice of holiness.

The neglect of the subject may be attributed to a variety of reasons, ranging from unscriptural notions to the wilful neglect of authentic, biblical holiness. Some entertain the mistaken notion that holiness is entirely optional in this earthly life. These appear to be heirs of a brand of first-century Gnosticism that viewed body and soul as separate entities, entirely unaffected by the other. The twentieth century "Gnostics" who are among evangelical ranks, will strongly aver that their "soul was saved" upon a past conversion experience, but they also assume any subsequent ill behavior in the mortal body is immaterial to their salvation. "Why should I worry with being holy now?" they might ask. "My soul is saved and I'm going to heaven, regardless of how I live on this earth."

Such thinking betrays their true spiritual condition, which is the tragic result of cheap grace. Genuine conversion involves our entire being—mind, body, and soul, and any profession of saving faith is simply spurious and presumptuous if it is not authenticated by a transformed life of obedience to Jesus as Lord (Matt. 7:21; 2 Cor. 5:17).

There are the more sincere folk who earnestly desire holiness but perceive it to be an ideal far exceeding their grasp. Some give a dispensational, futuristic interpretation to Jesus' Sermon on the Mount (Matt. 5—7), for example, and take it to be His code of ethics for our immortal, glorified life in the consummated Kingdom. Such a view relegates our present Christian life to complacency and conformity to the low standards of the unbelieving world, and consigns the Word of God to irrelevance.

Another unscriptural notion perceives the call to holiness as the call to sinless perfection, the complete eradication of the sin nature. These folks are too honest to claim this level of perfection for themselves but believe these false claims of their "superiors." True, there is an attainable level of spiritual maturity and totality of commitment that is essential for effective service in the kingdom of God (Eph. 4:13, Col. 1:28; 2 Tim. 3:17). This wholeness (Greek *telos*) is to be contrasted with the halfheartedness that shirks from the daily demands of discipleship, and is characterized by immaturity, confusion, distrust, and divided loyalty (Luke 9:61*ff;* Eph. 4:14; Jas. 1:6-8). This totality of commitment and essential spiritual maturity is not to be confused with sinless perfection.

At the point of conversion the dynamic process of salvation begins. We then begin to speak of having been saved at a time in the past, although it may be impossible for some of us to give the exact time and place of our conversion. There was an experience, regardless of the emotional impact, of our passing from death into life upon our trusting Christ as Savior and receiving Him as Lord (Eph. 2:5). This is our justification, our salvation past, our being put right with God by His grace through our faith in Jesus Christ (Rom. 5:1; Eph. 2:8-9).

From salvation past to the present moment another process has been at work—salvation present. The word for this dynamic process is sanctification, from the same root for holiness. The Greek word *hagios* means "separate," "separated," or "dedicated." The Israelites were called out from among the ungodly nations to be God's separate, distinctive people for His own use and to bear resemblance to His own character (Ex. 19:5*ff*). By His grace God has been at work in us, since the moment of our rebirth, to sanctify us as His chosen people, that we might be useful in His purposes (1 Pet. 2:9). Although we are already set apart and dedicated to Him (even the Old Testament sanctuary utensils were said to be sanctified in the sense of being *set apart* for God's use), yet the Holy Spirit has been at work in us to make us even more useful to God through this process of sanctification.

Because we still dwell in these earthly bodies, the downward pull of the old sin nature will have its effect. Scripture teaches us that, even as new creatures with the process of sanctification well under way, we cannot expect in this life to attain sinless perfection. We anticipate this perfection in salvation future, which is called glorification, the state of our being made sinlessly perfect, in the likeness of our Lord Jesus Christ (Rom. 8:30, 1 John 3:2-3). Christ has indeed called us to seek after His perfection, and we are enabled to live victoriously a life under the Spirit's control, useful to Him (Matt. 5:48; Rom. 8:1-8). J. Sidlow Baxter ably refuted the claims of sinless perfectionism and upheld the standard of our present "entire sanctification" (1 Thess. 5:23). Although our sinless perfection awaits salvation future we are now called to experience the sanctifying work of the Holy Spirit, "through and through" until we obtain our final redemption (Eph. 4:30).[2]

There is an element within Christianity which is often quite articulate in discounting the emphasis on holiness as being irrelevant to human and social concerns and impractical for day-to-day living. As James I. Packer pointed out, if the type of holiness propounded is a self-centered (rather than God and neighbor-centered) pursuit of "unbroken joy and tranquility" without thought of costly self-discipline, sacrifice, and suffering for Christ, *it is not biblical holiness,* even though it promises quick and practical solutions to life's problems.

> A quiet, sunny, tidy life without agony, free from distress at the quality of one's walk with God and one's work for others, is not what scripture tells us to aim at or expect. . . .[3]

True holiness is practical, not in a personally therapeutic sense, but as the only means of fulfilling our purpose to serve and glorify God. Holy lives are the only fit instruments "useful to the Master and prepared to do any good work" (2 Tim. 2:21).

Assuming, then, that the holiness proposed is biblically God-and-neighbor-oriented, there will still be those in and out of the church who will dismiss the subject as irrelevant and impractical. Even Christians fall prey to such naturalistic thinking that discounts the relevance of true spirituality to productive living and practical service to one's neighbor. As C. S. Lewis reminded us, an honest look at history shows that "the Christians who did most for the present world were just those who thought most of the next." The most significant social reform throughout history was borne on the wings of the church's spiritual vitality, under the leadership of those in pursuit both of personal holiness and social righteousness.[4] In his popular book, *Loving God,* Charles Colson shared how his pursuit of personal holiness led him of necessity into his work for social justice, his prison ministry, and his efforts in prison reform.

The misrepresentation of holiness has evoked still another judgement. Some mistakingly identify a life-negating, legalistic view of Christianity as holiness, and thereupon deem it undesirable. H. L. Mencken has perpetrated an unfair image of a Puritan as someone who has "the haunting fear that someone, somewhere may be happy." Indeed, there are dyspeptics in the ranks of Christianity who falsely equate their censorious, self-righteous, and proud spirit with genuine zeal for the Kingdom. But the seventeenth-century Puritans, and indeed all Christians of today who seek after true holiness, experience and affirm life to the full with all its joy and laughter.

I come now to suggest what I consider the main reason for the neglect of the pursuit of holiness, at least in the evangelical camp where I belong. Our theology will not allow us to say holiness is optional or unattainable. We must admit also it is not impractical or undesirable. However, because of certain excesses, associations, and misunderstandings surrounding this doctrine, holiness has become controversial. In our care to maintain our doctrinal equilibrium, we have refused to take up the substance of holiness, and as a result have become theological flyweights. We have maintained an evangelistic zeal in leading the lost to trust Christ as

Savior, but we have not done well in leading these converts to pursue holiness.

In the name of doctrinal purity, we have looked askance at Pentecostals, neo-charismatics and churches named "holiness," while neglecting ourselves to pursue the divine calling to true holiness. The credibility of our protestations of commitment to the authority of Scripture is based upon our willingness to take seriously all that it teaches including the command to holiness. The need of this hour and of every hour is courage for commitment to our God-given priorities and purpose as individuals, churches, and denominations. Perhaps our greatest danger is subtle self-diversion from the true practice of Christianity into endless debate and critique.

For one so strong in his theological positions, the great C. H. Spurgeon made a generous yet perceptive statement to the students in his preacher's college a century ago.

> I thought it no ill sign when the preaching of holiness was pushed even to an extreme. I trembled at the fanaticism, but I thanked God for the earnestness out of which it grew.

In our fear of extremes we have neglected the teaching and practice of holiness to the detriment of individual lives, and eventually unto the erosion of the vitality of our churches and denominational mission enterprise, all of which are fueled by the zeal and devotion of people serious about the call to a holy life.

Landrum Leavell, Southern Baptist leader and seminary president, bemoans the fact that someone can have "the morality of an average alley cat" and still be a member in good standing of the average Baptist church. In his denominational study book on the doctrine of the Holy Spirit, Dr. Leavell wrote that one cannot tell from the vocabulary or actions of a good many church members if they are saved or lost.[6] Equal to the need for biblical orthodoxy among Baptists and all Christians is the need for "orthopraxy"— that is, correct living as well as correct belief. Without our correct living, the world will not listen to our correct teaching and preaching. Also, without holiness within our ranks, expressing love, patience, and kindness toward one another, we will lose our identification before the world, our motivation for missions and evangelism, and our ability to minister to one another, including those with whom we disagree (John 13:34 *ff*). Whatever the past misunderstandings and causes of neglect, the present need is to hear and respond to the divine call to holiness. This is at the very heart of our purpose, which is to glorify God by what we are and what we do (1 Cor. 6:20).

Even in the evangelical world our *modus operandi* has been essentially activity-centered, and propelled by human-directed motivational gimmicks. The kind of work we are called to do, and the challenge facing Christianity at the end of the twentieth century, demands nothing less than the full power of the Holy Spirit, who resides in fullness only upon those who are serious about holiness. The famous frontiersman Davy Crockett may have—according to legend—gone bear hunting with only a switch, but we who call ourselves Christians, and are engaging in daily conflict with Satan, had better not attempt to do God's work with anything less than God's power that resides with those who seek after His holiness.

Biblical study and a serious attempt at biblical living soon yields the truth that what we are in terms of holiness is foundational to what we can do in terms of service. Regardless of our personal or institutional efficiency, sooner or later we will find ourselves unequal to the task. Before we attempt, like the proverbial little ram, to once again batter down the dam, we would do well to be certain we first answer the call to holiness. Thereupon we may discover God has a more useful, more productive work for us. And in the pursuit of holiness we will discover the recurring and increasing delight of hungering and thirsting for righteousness, which results in the filling and satisfaction of God's presence (Matt. 5:6; Eph. 3:14-19).

In these pages I wish to share with you several of the delightful truths I have learned in pursuit of holiness. This is not an exhaustive "how-to" manual by one who has in any sense "arrived" or mastered the subject. I ask you to join me, or rather let me join you, in your journey toward Christlikeness, and let me have the privilege of sharing truths God has made known from His Word, now being tried in my experience of walking with Him.

Any book on the subject of holiness of necessity must be selective and narrow in its scope since holiness is vitally and essentially related to the entire Christian life and responsibility. Succinctly stated, holiness is the life of God, and our lives are holy insofar as they reflect His life. Spurgeon observed that holiness is the visible side of Christianity. Our Lord Jesus Christ is "the exact representation" of God, the Word become flesh, and is our revealed standard for holiness (Heb. 1:3; John 1:14). Our calling is to be conformed to the likeness of the Son (Rom. 8:29).

Paul's portrayal of the fruit of the Spirit, those attributes that should characterize the life of the Christian who lives in step with the Holy Spirit, is also a good description of the character of our Lord Jesus (Gal. 5:22-23; 25). Although the Christlike virtues listed in these verses are by no means exhaustive of all we would say about the glorious character of Christ, or even of all the virtues of holiness mentioned in Scripture, yet we have in this listing of nine attributes a well-balanced portrayal of a holy life.

A structural choice and limited selection being necessary, I follow the pattern set by Sangster in *The Pure in Heart* as I seek to describe holiness through an exposition of Galatians 5:22*ff*. Because I wish to be helpful in a practical sense, I want to follow this eight-chapter description with three suggested steps to growth in holiness, with a final chapter on the church's call to holiness. But first, have you heard the call to holiness?

Notes

1. W. E. Sangster, *The Pure in Heart: A Study of Christian Sanctity* (London: The Epworth Press, 1954).

2. J. Sidlow Baxter, *Christian Holiness: Restudied and Restated* (Grand Rapids, Mich.: Zondervan Publishing House, 1977), pp. 147-158.

3. J. I. Packer, *Keep in Step with the Spirit* (Old Tappan, N.J.: Fleming H. Revell Co., 1984), p. 153.

4. C. S. Lewis, *Mere Christianity* (New York: MacMillan Publishing Co., 1952), p. 118.

5. C. H. Spurgeon, *An All-Round Ministry: Addresses to Ministers* and Students (Edinburgh: The Banner of Truth Trust, 1960), pp. 309-310.

6. Landrum P. Leavell, II, *The Doctrine of the Holy Spirit* (Nashville: Convention Press, 1983), pp. 40-41.

1
The Call to Holiness

Therefore, prepare your minds for action; be self-controlled; set your hope fully on the grace to be given you when Jesus Christ is revealed. As obedient children, do not conform to the evil desires you had when you lived in ignorance. But just as he who called you is holy, so be holy in all you do; for it is written: "Be holy, because I am holy" (1 Peter 1:13-16).

The urgency of this apostolic call to holiness is as potent today as it was in the first century. Peter wrote his epistle to encourage believers under threat of Roman persecution to remain steadfast in their calling to glorify God by the distinct and consistent witness of their transformed lives. We today who live in more congenial circumstances contend with the more subtle threat of cultural conformity with the godless, unbelieving world. A gradual erosion of on authentic, biblical life-style has dimmed the average Christian's understanding of, and consequently, desire for a life of holiness.

To many, holiness is either an odd life-style belonging to eccentric, sectarian Christianity (e.g., "holy-rollers"), or represents a level of piety attainable by only a relatively few "elite" Christians. This is illustrated by the way we typically use the appellation "saint" with a more Roman Catholic than biblical understanding. In the Roman church tradition, only the historic personage canonized by the heirarchy, with an impressive record of meritorious deeds including some miracles, has the right to be a saint. But Catholics are not the only ones with a select category for saints. My evangelical tradition tends to confer sainthood on well-known spiritual giants and assumes that special assignments in religious work, such as foreign missions, require a special level of saintliness.

Scripture, however, teaches us that all who belong to God through faith in Christ Jesus are HIs saints, His holy and sanctified ones. The words "saint" and "holy" and their derivatives are from the same Greek root (*hagios*). Even the immature, carnal Corinthian Christians were "sanctified in Christ Jesus and called to be holy"— i.e., saints (1 Cor. 1:2).

This misunderstanding and neglect of the biblical call to holiness has been detrimental to the cause of Christ ultimately and to the quality of Christian living directly. Unbelievers in the world today see little meaningful difference between their mindsets and life-styles than that of many professing Christians who supposedly have experienced transformation of life through a spiritual rebirth. Such a compromised Christianity has forfeited the right to bear witness to the world, and also is bereft of the spiritual dynamic necessary to experience the daily life of faith and obedience to which every Christian has been called.

Peter's admonition (1 Pet. 1:13-16) is based upon a quotation from Leviticus 11:45, and includes the address, authority, and aim of the call to holiness.

The Address of the Call

The call to be holy was directed by the apostle to God's elect ". . . scattered throughout Pontus, Galatia, Cappadocia, Asia, and Bithynia," and as God's eternal word, is addressed to all God's elect "who have been chosen according to the foreknowledge of God the Father, through the sanctifying work of the Spirit. . . ." (1 Pet. 1:1-2). After his opening salutation, Peter gave praise to God for the living hope He has given to all who have experienced the new birth (verses 3-12). This declaration of God's gracious provision of salvation through faith in Jesus Christ is in the indicative mood, but beginning with our text, verses 13-16, these action verbs change to the imperative mood. After recounting what God has done for us (indicative), Peter said what we, in grateful response to God's grace, must do (imperative), which is to "be holy in all [we] do." We are to be holy because He is holy.

Every child of God is saved by grace, having been justified by faith in Jesus Christ. Justification is a completed transaction, and in this "past tense" of the concept of salvation we cannot be any more saved than we are right now. We have been saved by God's grace. Yet, we are also being sanctified by grace. The rebirth experience includes justification, but also initiates the life-long process of sanctification. The moment we receive Christ as Savior and Lord, the Holy Spirit enters our lives and baptizes us into the Body of Christ, and transforms our innermost nature (2 Cor. 5:17). The Holy Spirit sets us apart (i.e., sanctifies us) as a newborn child of God (Rom. 15:16).

Sanctification as a "setting apart" from the unregenerate, unbelieving world is as decisive and irrevocable as justification. Yet, unlike justification, sanctification is a gradual process by which the indwelling Holy Spirit changes us more and more into the likeness of Jesus Christ (2 Cor. 3:18). The Holy Spirit who initiates and effects our rebirth (Titus 3:5) remains as a permanent resident in our lives, the Guarantor of our salvation (Rom. 8:9; Eph. 1:13-14). He continues the life-long process of sanctifying us, enabling us to grow in holiness, without which "no one will see the Lord." Unless this holiness-producing Presence is within us, we cannot claim to be the children of God (Heb. 12:14).

Thus, for the Christian to deny that the call to holiness includes him or her is to renounce any claims to be a child of God. Holiness is every Christian's calling, since every genuine Christian has been saved (justified, i.e., put right with God) and is being saved (sanctified, i.e., made more and more into the likeness of Jesus Christ).

This call to holiness reveals the New Testament balance of gift and demand. Salvation is totally initiated by God, and only because of His grace can we even believe so as to be saved (Eph. 2:8-9). But once His grace stirs and awakens the conscience to believe, we must exercise faith, repentance, and trust. Now that we have become God's children of grace—His workmanship—we must fulfill His purpose in our new creation, which is to do the good works "God prepared in advance for us to do," and "put on the new self, created to be like God in true righteousness and holiness" (Eph. 2:10; 4:24). "His divine power has given us everything we need for life and godliness," Peter said, but we must make every effort to add to our faith all the virtues of a holy, Christlike life (2 Pet. 1:3-7). His gracious provisions for a holy life demand that we obey His commands for obedient, godly living.

God graciously provided for our holiness, but we must hear and heed the call, and make holiness our task. The imagery Peter used (1 Pet. 1:13-16) is that of a runner in ancient times, who gathers up his long, flowing robe and tucks it under his belt in order to run freely. We use the equivalent expression: "Roll up your sleeves and go to work." Thus, I might paraphrase this verse to show our responsibility in hearing the call to holiness: "Roll up the sleeves of your mind and get ready for action" (1 Pet. 1:13).

If you haven't heard the call, you simply are not listening. God Himself is calling.

The Authority of the Call

The widespread absence of holy living today is perhaps explained in part by a misunderstanding of holiness as every Christian's calling. But sadly, the problem is deeper than ignorance. Many professing Christians know their lives are not pleasing to God, yet are not willing to repent of worldliness and disobedience. This spiritual indifference is indicative of the need for a renewal of a deep reverence for God and regard for His authority. This need is apparent within evangelical Christianity and among Bible-believing denominations of those who claim to be "a people of the Book." Those who adhere to belief in the inspiration and authority of Scripture and yet fail or refuse to obey direct commandments regarding holiness of life and conduct are being inconsistent, if not hypocritical.

The call to be holy is the command of the Almighty, who Himself is perfect in holiness, the standard of holiness. Jesus Christ, who is "the exact representation" of God (Heb. 1:3), is the description of perfect holiness. To be holy is to be like Jesus Christ, God's Son.

Something of the holiness of God is perhaps included in His awesome majesty, His transcendent otherness and unapproachableness, as Rudolf Otto explained in his well-known book, *The Idea of the Holy*. Throughout the written Word, the holiness of God is declared by psalm, proclamation, and testimony of those who "worship the Lord in the splendor of his holiness" (Ps. 29:2b). Even the best of men, like Moses, Job, Isaiah, and Daniel were smitten with their sinfulness and unworthiness in the light of God's holiness. Though He clothed Himself in human flesh and His transcendent glory was veiled (except at exceptional manifestations, such as His Transfiguration), the Lord Jesus inspired the humble acknowledgement of His holiness and majestic power (Luke 5:8).

The God who is Himself perfectly holy, who is perfect in His moral character, whose presence is unapproachable light, glory, and majesty, is the One who calls us to be holy. Jesus, the Lamb of God, who purchased us with His blood and made us to be a kingdom of priests to serve our God, is worthy to receive all honor and glory and praise (Rev. 5:9-12). He has called us to be holy, to glorify Him by fulfilling our calling to share His very nature.

From the very formation of His chosen people, God gave His absolute moral law, the Ten Commandments, which reflected His own character and expressed His demands for His people. The Old Testament is an exposé of Israel's failure to attain to God's moral requirements to be holy as He is holy (Lev. 11:44). Jesus Christ, God's Son, was sent to be the fulfillment of the demands of the law, to show by His life what the law demands. But Jesus' primary purpose was to die for sinners a substitutionary death, which would satisfy the just demands of the law of our holy God (John 12:27; 1 Tim. 1:15). God restores the lost relationship with us, broken by sin, as we receive Christ as Savior and Lord. By His grace, He then removes from us the penalty we have incurred by our own sin (Rom. 5:1;10).

We are free from the judgment of the law, yet we are not free from God's command that we fulfill the demands of the moral law. True Christian liberty is the freedom through the power of the Holy Spirit to live a holy, obedient life of righteousness that is more than refraining from prohibitions, such as the sixth commandment against murder. In His Sermon on the Mount, Jesus taught that His followers must not only refrain from murder, but must avoid unjustified anger or malice. Indeed, the Christian is to fulfill the royal law of absolute love for God and for his neighbor, with not only moral restraint but with positive, caring behavior and active concern (Matt. 5:21-26; Jas. 2:8).

The Aim of the Call

What a high calling is this call to holiness, to share in the very nature of God and to become more and more like Jesus Christ Himself (Rom. 8:29)!

We have noted that the call to holiness is issued the moment we receive Christ as Savior. The process of sanctification begins at the point of justification, when upon our repentance from sin we are put right with God. The Holy Spirit continues this work of making us holy as we daily obey the Word of God, which instructs and guides us as we strive to be holy, as we bring our character and conduct into conformity with God's will. Later in our study we will consider some of the practical steps to holiness, such as prayer, personal and corporate worship and Christian fellowship, daily obedience to God's will, and conscious abiding in His full presence.

At this juncture we should recognize that the aim of the call to holiness is that we seek to bring all of our being under the gracious influence of the Holy Spirit, who desires to sanctify us "through and through" (1 Thess. 5:23). It is God's will and our present responsibility that we bring every aspect of our lives, behavior, and relationships, under the conscious influence of the Holy Spirit. In this way we can reach spiritual maturity and be useful in God's service (Eph. 4:13).

This, of course, does not mean we will in this life reach a level of sinless perfection. Later, in our study, we will consider the warfare of our new nature in the Holy Spirit against the old sinful nature that remains in our bodies of flesh, "the battleground of Satan." There is to be, nevertheless, progressive growth toward spiritual perfection. In His Sermon on the Mount, Jesus gave us nothing less than this standard of perfection as our goal toward which we should progress (Matt. 5:48). The apostle Paul, even as an aged, tried, and true missionary to the world, expressed his determination to reach "the goal to win the prize for which God has called me heavenward in Christ Jesus" (Phil. 3:14). The aim of the call to holiness is to fulfil His purpose for us to be not only entirely sanctified, but sinlessly perfect. Of course, we cannot attain perfection in this life, but the presence of Christ in us is our hope of the future glory of sinless perfection (Col. 1:27).

Salvation past (justification) and salvation present (sanctification) are the guarantee that the process will be consummated in salvation future, which is glorification (Phil. 1:6). Someday, when we either depart to be with the Lord or He appears in His glorious second coming, our salvation will be complete. "But we know that when He appears, we shall be like Him, for we shall see Him as He is" (1 John 3:2b). Knowing that complete Christlikeness is our calling and destiny, we should begin now living up to our heavenward calling (1 John 3:3). Since the world about us, with its downward pull, is destined for destruction, "What kind of people ought you to be?" asked Peter. In answer to his own question he said, "You ought to live holy and godly lives as you look forward to the day of God and speed its coming" (2 Pet. 3:11-12).

In the next eight chapters we will consider the beautiful and balanced life of holiness described by Paul as "the fruit of the Spirit" (Galatians 5:22-23). It's the kind of life God desires to give to all His children, and to this life He has called us.

The call of God is both the measure and motivation for our holiness. We are called to be holy in the same way He is holy, as revealed in Jesus Christ, and also because He is holy and He has commanded us, His children, to resemble Him in character.

In his commentary on this text, Baptist theologian Ray Summers noted that the central idea is expressed in verse sixteen, the quotation from Leviticus 11:45, "You shall therefore be holy, for I am holy." In the Leviticus passage, wrote Summers, "the motivation for holiness on the part of God's people (Israel) was that he who had redeemed them from the bondage of Egypt was a holy God. They, as his people, were therefore to be a holy people—like God, like people." Summers continues:

> Peter used the same argument for the Christians as the new Israel. The God who had redeemed them from their pagan life was a holy God. They, as the redeemed, were to be like their God—holy.[1]

We have all received the same call from God "who has saved us and called us to a holy life—not because of anything we have done but because of his own purpose and grace" (2 Tim. 1:9). What a great privilege and responsibility, to be called to a life of holiness, and to live in such a way to fulfil the will of God and be an answer to the prayer of the Lord Jesus Himself who prayed that we might be "truly sanctified," sharing His very nature (John 17:19).

The call of God came to the boy Samuel, who mistook the divine call for the voice of Eli. Clearly and repeatedly God has been calling us to become distinctly His holy people. Either because of inattention or unwillingness we have either not recognized the voice as God's voice, or have said to ourselves, "He's talking to somebody else."

Make no mistake about it. God Himself is calling you and me. Now is the time to listen again to His call, and like Samuel, respond by saying, "Speak, for your servant is listening" (1 Sam. 3:10).

Note

1. Ray Summers, *The Broadman Bible Commentary* (Nashville: Broadman Press, 1972), p. 152.

2

Holiness Is Love

But the fruit of the Spirit is *love*. . . . (Gal. 5:22).

Love is patient, love is kind. It does not envy, it does not boast, it is not proud. It is not rude, it is not self-seeking, it is not easily angered, it keeps no record of wrongs. Love does not delight in evil but rejoices with the truth. It always protects, always trusts, always hopes, always perseveres. (1 Cor. 13:4-7).

Dear friends, let us love one another, for love comes from God. Everyone who loves has been born of God and knows God. Whoever does not love does not know God, because God is love.(1 John 4:7-8).

Holiness is every Christian's calling, but what does it mean to be holy? I am convinced that the call to holiness is virtually the summation of the entire Christian experience. If we answer the call and obey the command to be holy we will essentially satisfy the demands of our Christian commitment. My study of holiness has moved me away from a narrowly defined, passive notion that to be holy one has only to refrain from certain negative behavior. Holiness, as I am beginning to understand it, demands rigorous spiritual self-discipline and a life of active service to the cause of Christ. To be holy is to be like Jesus Christ and to obey His commands, which involve my personal character behavior and also my responsibility to others. The basic, Christlike virtues that should determine both our character and conduct are represented in Paul's description of the fruit of the Spirit (Gal. 5:22-23).

28

In his letter to the Galatians, Paul issued his great "emancipation proclamation," warning Christians who were under Christian freedom to be wary of any who would lead them into spiritual bondage. The essence of freedom, Paul said in 5:13-26, is to live under the influence of the Holy Spirit, who liberates us from the bondage of sin and the condemnation of the law. Positively speaking, Paul showed that as we live under the influence of the Holy Spirit we fulfil God's Moral Law, which is summarized in a single command: "Love your neighbor as yourself" (Gal. 5:14).

Instead of being dominated by the passions of the sinful nature, which result in sordid, destructive behavior characteristic of the unconverted life (vv. 19-21), we now are free to experience the divine, supernatural influence of the Holy Spirit, who produces in our lives those Jesus-like characteristics Paul described as the fruit of the Spirit (verses 22-23). Although these virtues are not an exhaustive list, they provide a balanced description of the character of our Lord Jesus, which serves as the paradigm of every Christian's calling (Rom. 8:29).

Paul did not describe these characteristics as the fruits of the Spirit, plural, but used the singular to emphasize the unitive nature of these Christlike graces, which are like grapes linked inseparably together in one cluster. The Holy Spirit does not give us just one, but as we live under His influence, He blesses us with the whole cluster of graces.The indwelling Spirit gives every believer all nine virtues, though at times when our human weakness dominates, one or more may be less than apparent.

At the head of the list is love, which Paul has already described in this section as the essence of the law. The Royal Law contains the first and second greatest commandments, and embody the fulfillment of all our obligations to God and to others. Jesus said,

> "Love the Lord your God with all your heart and with all your soul and with all your mind. This is the first and greatest commandment. And the second is like it: Love your neighbor as yourself. All the

Law and the Prophets hang on these two commandments." (Matt. 22:37-40).

Love may be viewed as the branches that hold together the grapes of the cluster, or perhaps better, love is not as much a separate grace as it is the dominant essence of the other virtues. Should you taste each grape of this cluster of the fruit of the Spirit, each would have a distinctive flavor, but all would share the sweetness of love. Indeed, J. Sidlow Baxter said, "the spiritual protoplasm from which all true experience of sanctification develops is our love to Christ," and "when we earnestly love Him, everything else falls into its proper place and our Lord suffuses us with this sanctifying Spirit."[1]

Paul himself expressed this unifying nature of love, saying that "over all these virtues put on love, which binds them all together in perfect unity" (Col. 3:14). In his magnificent "hymn to love" in 1 Corinthians 13, Paul portrayed love as the grand virtue which is the sum total of the other virtues of the Christian life (vv. 4-7), and is the "sine qua non" of both the life of the believer and the life of the church. As we will discover in our study of the other eight virtues of holiness, all are motivated and sustained by love, but first we must understand the distinctiveness of love.

Love Is Distinct

A deficiency in the English language requires that we properly understand the nature of the love that defines holiness. We use the same word "love" to express a tremendous range of experiences, from the basest sort of pleasure to the highest kind of commitment. We say we "love" homemade ice cream, the Dallas Cowboys, and we "love" to take a walk in the park. Obviously, we are expressing our delight in certain experiences. We also use the same word to express our devotion to our family and friends, and to translate the Bible verse, John 3:16, that expresses God's greatest gift to mankind. The first-century everyday Greek language, on the other hand, employed four words of sharper focus. The Greeks would use the word *storgé* for affection-love, expressed particularly among family members. It is such a basic, natural affection that even the animal world might experience it. It is as natural for a human mother to lovingly care for her baby as for a mother cat to protect her kittens.

The word *philos* describes the friendship kind of love that is also referred to as fellowship and companionship. Friendship is a priceless gift so lacking in today's impersonal society. Today's residents of Philadelphia probably have no idea they live in the "City of Brotherly Love."

Eros is romantic love that includes physical, sexual expression. The romantic concepts of love popularized by today's media employ exclusively this eros concept, and cheapen and distort the physical aspect of love.

All of these three concepts are legitimate, God-given expressions of human love. In the Spirit-directed life of holiness, these loves can find their highest fulfillment and are kept in proper perspective. The fourth love is *agape*—divine love, the unique love, the biblically revealed love. *Agape* is the love God has for us and requires us to have for one another, and the love that gives the other loves their proper expression and fulfillment.

C. S. Lewis distinguished between need-love and gift-love. The first three are need-loves. We love in these ways because of our various human needs. But God's love for us, expressed in the gospel story, is a gift-love. In a real sense, only God is capable of gift-love. He alone needs nothing. He enables and commands that we enter into the experience of His *agapē* love, and that we love God and others with the same kind of love. Even so, said Lewis, when we love God and others, it is because of our need. But we can and do enter into that experience of *agapē*, God-like, giving love, which Jesus said distinguishes His followers from everyone else who cannot know that love apart from grace.[2] Thus, this unique *agapē* love is not only the unitive grace, but also is the distinguishing mark of the Christian and church (John 13:35). When we truly love, we are most like God, who is the essence of holiness.

Love Is Godly

John, who is referred to as "The Apostle of Love," wrote his First Epistle so his readers might have assurance of eternal life (1 John 5:13). We know we have eternal life if our faith passes John's three tests—the moral, doctrinal, and social. The moral test requires we no longer continue practicing sin the way we did in our lost condition. The doctrinal test demands we believe in the divine/human nature of the Incarnate Christ. The third is the social test, requiring our love for one another.[3]

One passage giving this love test is 1 John 4:7-21, which explains that *agapē* love is essential to God, the Christian, and for our witness to the world. Love is essential to God in the sense that *agapē* love characterizes and expresses His very being. This gift-love is endemic to the nature of God, who needs nothing but chooses to give. Paul Scherer said the words "God is love" (1 John 4:8b) do not define God but rather define *agapē* love.[4] We can avow much more about God, such as "God is almighty," but when we affirm that God is love we have said all we could possibly say about love. God revealed Himself fully in Jesus Christ, and the Christ event was the quintessential expression of gift-love (John 3:16; Rom. 5:8).[3]

In this dissertation on love, John argued that, since we Christians are born of God, are in fact His children, then love is essential and latent to our new nature (verses 7-12). The Spirit of the God who is love is the same One who dwells within each of us (verse 13). So characteristically essential is this love, John declared, that it is impossible to know God and not express this gift-love (verse 8). The expression of this love is not primarily verbal, but active and practical. God's gift-love in Christ was active and effective for our eternal well-being, and so His gift-love in us finds expression in sacrificial and practical ways.

Maybe you have heard about the minister who spent his day off pouring a concrete driveway. That evening he sat on the front porch with his wife. While admiring the results of his hard day's work, this preacher reviewed with his wife his upcoming Sunday morning's sermon on Jesus and little children, and the importance of our loving children. Suddenly, some neighborhood boys, pursuing a football, came running through his freshly poured concrete driveway. The preacher, shouting in anger, grabbed the boys, and demanded they make restitution for his damaged driveway. His wife, intervening in behalf of the terrified boys, reminded him of his sermon on loving children. "I love them in the abstract," he explained, "but not in the concrete!"

Legitimate, God-like love is always in the concrete. The parable of the Good Samaritan is Jesus' response to a query about eternal life. If we know God savingly, we will respond to the needs of our neighbor, as did the Samaritan, whose active involvement with the victim was evidence of eternal life (Luke 10:25-37). John wrote,

> This is how we know what love is: Jesus Christ laid down his life for us. And we ought to lay down our lives for our brothers. If anyone has material possessions and sees his brother in need but has no pity on him, how can the love of God be in him? Dear children, let us not love with words or tongue but with actions and in truth. (1 John 3:16-18).

Although John addressed primarily our responsibility to love our fellow Christians, he was also aware of our responsibility to the world. *Agapē* love is essential to God and to the Christian in an internal, characteristic sense, but to the world love is essential in a ministry sense. The title of a popular song of the 60's, "What the World Needs Now Is Love, Sweet Love," is still apropos. The world does not, however, need a sweet, sentimental, romantic love, but needs the active, giving love of God, received through saving faith in Christ and disseminated by followers of Jesus who care about one another and minister to the needs of a hurting world.

With the grace of love, as perhaps with no other of the fruit of the Spirit, we see the social dimension of holiness. To be holy is not to focus on self-improvement, but rather to die to self-interest and become involved in the needs of others. We desire to be like Jesus Christ, not for self-aggrandizement, but that He might be made known through us, and that we might with authority be His witnesses and servants in the world.

Divine love was the motivation for the incarnation and the cross (John 3:16). In the same way, Christ's indwelling love becomes our motivation to evangelize the lost and to fulfil the mission of Christ to the world (2 Cor. 5:14).

In the first chapter of his Gospel, John declared "No one has ever seen God," followed by a statement of purpose regarding the incarnation: . . . "but God the only Son, who is at the Father's side, has made him known" (John 1:18). John repeated this preliminary truth in his First Epistle, and followed with another statement of purpose: "No one has ever seen God; but if we love each other, God lives in us and His love is made complete in us" (1 John 4:12). It seems as though John recognized that in a real way we who are followers of Jesus are an incarnation of God. Jesus was the perfect incarnation, but we are, as His followers, to so love one another that today's world will be able to see the authenticity and reality of God. As we have already noted, Jesus taught that our love for one another would distinguish us before the world as His followers, and as we love one another sacrificially and all persons unconditionally, we are acting the most like God. In fact, to love as He commands us to love demands that we depend on His grace and let Him love through us.

It is against human nature to love our enemies, and to do good to those who insult and persecute us, yet our Lord has so commanded us because this is how the world will know we are children of the Heavenly Father (Matt. 5:11*ff*, 43*ff*). Not by our human resolve or strength can we love as Jesus commanded, but only by the will and power of His Spirit working through us (Phil. 2:13). It was the Spirit Himself who gave Paul the compassion to enable him to be willing to be cut off from Christ for the sake of his kinsmen's salvation (Rom. 9:3). This kind of compassion, which Paul had witnessed before his conversion in the martyrdom of Stephen, no doubt made a tremendous impression on him. As Paul (then Saul of Tarsus) approvingly watched the horrible execution he heard Stephen's compassionate prayer of forgiveness, "Lord, do not hold this sin against them" (Acts 7:60). Stephen's *agapē* love was impressive because it was so Christlike, closely approximating our Lord's crucifixion prayer of forgiveness, "Father, forgive them, for they do not know what they are doing" (Luke 23:34).

Though now nearly two millennia separate us from the incarnation, the witness of *agapē* love continues to impress the world through people such as Elisabeth Elliot, whose sacrificial love was poured out upon those who had brutally murdered her missionary husband.[5] For most of us, the opportunity to express our love through intense suffering of injustice or martyrdom may never come. Yet all of us have daily opportunities to love in ways that indicate a genuinely Christlike concern for others, especially those in the family of God (Gal. 6:10).

Agapē love is particularly Godly love because it is, in the words of Lewis, a gift-love. God does not have needs, but has chosen to love us by meeting our needs. He allows those of us who have savingly experienced His love in Christ to express that same kind of *agapē*, gift-love. As Lewis said, for us *agapē* is not entirely a gift-love because we need to experience and to express it to find our own personal fulfillment and to be obedient to God. But it is the highest love. Though it does not replace the other need-loves, it keeps them in their proper place and increases the meaning and value of the lesser loves. When the love of Christ dwells in us richly, we are willing and able to express family affection, find our own personal fulfillment and to be obedient to God. But it is the highest love and, though it does not replace the other need-loves, it keeps them in their proper place and increases the meaning and value of the lesser loves. When the love of Christ dwells in us richly, we are willing and able to express family affection, strengthen and maintain relationships of deep and abiding friendship, and we are free to pursue romantic love as it culminates in the God-given relationships of marriage.

By the way, many marriage problems demand the solution of *agapē* love. If the romance is gone, in most cases it can be restored by the discipline and determination of *agapē,* giving love. If couples, supposedly "out-of-love" for each other would resolve to love God, they could then love one another again. To love God is to obey Him (John 14:15). If couples obeyed God by honoring the marriage vow, then expressed love by meeting the needs of one another, then the emotional side of love would be restored. Real love is much more than romantic, though most couples could stand a little more romance! Love seeks to give to the other, regardless of the marriage partner's response.

All the lesser loves, thus, are ruled by the highest love, *agapē,* which is the crowning, unifying virtue of all the other characteristics of holiness. If we don't have this love, we don't have anything of Godliness, no matter how noble and enlightened our lives may appear (1 Cor. 13:1-3). The fruit of the Spirit, the life of holiness, is first of all love.

Notes

1. J. Sidlow Baxter, *Going Deeper* (Grand Rapids, Mich.: Zondervan Publishing House, 1959), pp. 132-133.

2. C. S. Lewis, *The Four Loves* (New York: Harcourt Brace Jovanovich, Inc., 1960), pp. 175-186.

3. James Montgomery Boice, *The Epistles of John* (Grand Rapids, Mich.: Zondervan Publishing House, 1981), p. 14.

4. Paul Scherer, *The Word God Sent* (New York: Harper and Row, Publishers, 1965), pp. 225-233.

5. Elisabeth Elliot, *Through Gates of Splendor* (New York: Harper and Row, Publishers, 1958),

3

Holiness Is Joy

the fruit of the Spirit is . . . joy (Gal. 5:22).
you will fill me with joy in your presence (Ps. 16:11)
Rejoice in the Lord always. I will say it again: Rejoice! (Phil. 4:4).

Few would think of joy when describing characteristics of holiness. We are likely to confine our thoughts of holiness to concepts of self-denial and burdensome discipline and duty. We think of joy as perhaps an occasional mood of exhilaration prompted by delightful or festive circumstances and happy friends. Yet, as we shall see, joy (the Greek, *chara*) is a vital part of the life of holiness, and is an important aspect of the life of obedient faith. The summons and even frequent command to rejoice appears one hundred ninety times in the Bible and seventy times in the New Testament alone. Joy is presented as a discipline unique to the Christian life rather than a capricious mood likely to strike only the lucky. As was true for C. S. Lewis, joy may allure us to faith, but only through a personal relationship with Christ can we know joy as an integral and dependable part of our life.[1]

Christian joy is a finely-tuned kind of thing, and false imitations of joy sound badly out of tune. Even in Christian circles there are the superficial superstars of the faith, who would lead you to believe they always lived one thousand miles from, not only the nearest source of sin, but from the nearest cause of sadness or defeat. Through their forced smiles they always manage a "Praise

38

the Lord," or "God bless you, brother" when perhaps a word of confession or an honest expression of need would be more appropriate. The Christian life faces the realities of life, expressing both delight and disappointment, exhilaration and grief, concern and praise (Jas. 5:13; Rom. 12:15; Eccl. 3:4).

Perhaps even Christians confuse happiness with joy. God does not command happiness, which is an entirely human mood of delight dependent on fortuitous circumstances. Happiness depends on what happens, but joy is a gift from God and a command of God. Because real joy is misunderstood, joyful Christians are often misunderstood. The world doesn't understand how a grieving widow can rejoice in her hope in Christ, and find grace for laughter even through the veil of her tears. The Franciscans were reprimanded for laughing in church, and the early Methodists were censured for borrowing their happy gospel tunes from the dance hall. These, like their modern-day counterparts, refuse to believe God is a dour deity who demands a life of delightless discipline. The world, which knows only its undependable moments of happiness, needs to see evidence in the lives of Christians of a joy that is God-given, always growing, and infinitely greater than the world's imitations.

Given Joy

The believer's joy is part and parcel of his new life in the Spirit through the rebirth experience. Instead of being condemned to the destructive works of the old sin nature, we are set free to live by the Spirit and to enjoy the whole cluster of the fruit of the Spirit, including joy (Gal. 5:22). God fully gives His gift of joy to His children, who are born by the Holy Spirit and receive the power of the Spirit (Rom. 15:13). Although we must be careful not to impose the same emotional expectations on everyone, yet the experience of rebirth will necessarily introduce the joy of a newfound peace with God and the newly-received gift of eternal life.

Perhaps this joy is closely akin to the sense of peace and gratitude, but joy seems also to usher in a release of the human spirit, which may range from a calm rising of spiritual energy to an outburst of exhilaration and celebration, as with the healed cripple (Acts 3:8*ff*). Perhaps "gusto" is closer to the New Testament concept of joy than is the word happiness, which is often fragile and fleeting. However reserved or effervescent a particular personality, the life-changing experience of being converted from death to eternal life will occasion the kind of joy that filled the whole family of the Philippian jailer (Acts 16:34).

Jesus cautioned the seventy-two against focusing their joy upon their newfound ministerial success (that even the demons were submitting to their authority), which is a modern-day ministerial tendency to which I can attest. Jesus declared that we are to instead rejoice that our names are written in heaven (Luke 10:17-20). Times of ministerial or other kinds of success will wax and wane, but we can always rejoice in the fact that our names are written in heaven. We must never "outgrow" this initial joy given the moment we first believed and were received through the gates of new life.

Joy is a gift but also a demand, a grace but also a discipline. We are given the fruit of joy, but we ourselves must nurture the growth of joy as we cultivate those qualities which make make for joy. Paul wrote his Philippian epistle of joy while in a Roman prison. Throughout this encouraging letter, he admonished, "rejoice in the Lord." He knew, from his own experiences of hardship and adversity, that *we cannot rejoice in our circumstances* because we cannot depend on their congeniality or on the cooperation of others. *We can, however, rejoice in the Lord,* even as we can depend on His presence. In His presence He fills us with joy (Ps. 16:11), a joy we first knew the moment we were born again and became children of God.

Growing Joy

Perhaps for many Christians their conversion experience was the most joyful time of their life. This rebirth, of course, is the most crucial moment and the greatest transition in human experience. Jesus told us of the rejoicing of the angels of God over one sinner who repents (Luke 15:7,10). If heaven's joy in our conversion is the joy of recovery, then the convert's is the joy of discovery. When Andrew witnessed to his brother, Simon Peter, he declared, "Eureka," we have discovered Him (John 1:41)! Jesus compared the joy of salvation to the discovery of a great treasure (Matt. 13:44).

Great is this initial joy, it is the will of the Father that the joy of His children increase. Jesus enjoins us to abide in Him in an everincreasing fellowship of love, obedience and prayer, like a branch abides in the vine, that our joy might be complete, that we might know the same joy He experiences in His perfect fellowship with the Heavenly Father.

For joy to grow we must remove all self-erected limitations and barriers to joy. Before he could ask God to restore to him the lost joy of his salvation, David had first of all to confess his sin and experience the removal of his joy-robbing sense of guilt and shame (Ps. 51:1-12). Because God is infinitely loving and zealous for our spiritual well-being, He will chasten us for His purposes of our discipline and restoration to His will (Heb. 12:4-11). If our lives are not pleasing to Him, we will forfeit the joy of His fellowship. No true child of God wants to go on in that miserably joyless condition. We have only to confess and forsake whatever the sin, however flagrant or secret. Inner sins of attitude (i.e. pride, indifference), spirit (i.e. rebellion, fear, envy, jealousy), or thoughts (i.e. lust, greed, anxiety) will rob us of joy, but will be forgiven and overcome by our forgiving, gracious heavenly Father (1 John 1:9; Gal. 5:16).

In a real sense, joy in itself is a part of holiness but also a by-product of all other aspects of holiness. As we discipline ourselves to experience the victorious power of the Holy Spirit, in overcoming the desires of the old sinful nature, we are released to experience the joy of holiness. It is the joy of a sustained fellowship with the Heavenly Father. Our sins, whether inward or outward transgressions, are barriers to fellowship and usefulness; they grieve the indwelling Holy Spirit (Isa. 59:1-2, Eph. 4:30). We cannot experience much joy if our divine guest, the Holy Spirit, is saddened by our disobedience.

Just as joy is released as sins are confessed and forsaken, so is joy increased as we grow in our fellowship with God through obedience to His commands and conformity to His character.[2] Jesus emphasized that as we obey His commands we experience His love and the fullness of His joy (John 15:9-11). For happiness, we are passively at the mercy of our circumstances, but as children of God we are actively to pursue joy in the Lord always (Phil. 4:4). As we draw near to God in heartfelt prayer and moment-by-moment awareness of His presence, we experience joy (Ps. 16:11; Phil. 4:5b).[3]

We can determine to experience God-given joy, even when times are hardest. Jesus promised that no one, not even our persecutors, could ever rob us of His joy (John 16:22). The persecuted apostles rejoiced, not in spite of their suffering, but rather "because they had been counted worthy of suffering disgrace for the Name" (Acts 5:41). Indeed, potential sorrow is turned into joy for the child of God who obeys and communes with the loving, Heavenly Father. In times of adversity that joy-instilling fellowship with Christ is intensified. As the song says, "He gives more grace when the burdens grow greater." Those same apostles who experienced such persecution are the ones who admonish us to rejoice in our sufferings, and go on to explain that God has a purpose for our lives, even in His permitting adversity and hardship.

As we face these trials with the perspective of faith, we see God's design to develop in us the qualities of perseverance, patience, mature character, and hope (Jas. 1:2-4; Rom. 5:3-5). Our suffering occasioned by our lives of holy living and courageous witness should occasion our rejoicing in the privilege of participating in the suffering of Christ and in the assurance that His Spirit rests upon us and we will for eternity share His glory (1 Pet. 4:12-14).

No one except a masochist enjoys suffering in itself, but the Christian is enabled to see the bigger purpose God has in allowing suffering. We know the sovereign God limits even what Satan would do to afflict us, as is revealed in the "behind-the-scenes" drama in Job's experience (Job 1:1 to 2:10). During the fiery ordeal it is hard to gain a spiritual perspective on suffering. I may not praise the Lord while changing my flat tire, but on later reflection, I can rejoice in the perfect providence of the God who in all things "works for the good of those who love him" (Rom. 8:28). Joseph no doubt smarted from the terrible injustices suffered at the hands of his brothers, yet, by the perspective gained from his faith in the God of providential love, was able to forgive and restore his brothers, thus celebrating the fulfillment of God's purpose of his life in "the saving of many lives" (Gen. 50:20).

In a university gymnasium where I frequently exercised was (by the weight-lifting machines) a sign with a concise but spiritually applicable message: "No pain, no gain." Just as muscle tissue develops only by bodily exertion against stout resistence, so spiritual character and genuine holiness result from adversity, and would-be sorrow turns to joy in the growth and development of godliness. Joy is holiness and joy grows with holiness.

The amazing missionary statesman E. Stanley Jones noted that Christian joy is "joy with its sleeves rolled up." This means a joy in the midst of active service. Joy is the gusto of giving ourselves away, the joyous dynamic of the exchanged life. Jesus said if we lose our self-serving life for His sake we will gain His eternal, abundant life (Matt. 16:24-26). The life of taking up our cross and following Jesus is a life that is filled with the joy of His strength.

Nehemiah reminded the people after their gigantic rebuilding project that the joy of the Lord was their strength (Neh. 8:10c). When we find and do the ministry God has for us, He sustains and strengthens us with His joyous presence.

An example of this dynamic can be seen in the life of our Lord Jesus, who sat physically exhausted and hungry at Jacob's Well. When the Samaritan woman came to draw water, Jesus began to minister to her spiritual thirst. It appears that this encounter which transformed the woman into an evangelist to the city of Sychar also ministered to Jesus' need for refreshment. When the disciples returned with food supplies, Jesus appeared refreshed by the food they knew nothing about (John 4:32). The joy of service and the joy of fruit-bearing had been our Lord's strength.

Jesus told us that if we would abide in Him as branches in the vine, we would experience the joy of bearing fruit (John 15:16). The spiritual fruit that refreshes and gives joy includes our personal holiness, the fruit of the Spirit (Gal. 5:22-23), but also lives that are reached for Christ as a result of our godly living, the witness of our good works, and our efforts in personal evangelism (see Matt. 5:16; Eph. 2:10; John 15:16; Rom. 1:13).

Paul rejoiced in the fruit of his ministry, those who had become his spiritual "children," his "joy and crown," as they accepted the gospel he preached (1 Thess. 2:19 *ff*). This joy of the harvest is our strength to continue the efforts of sowing the seed of a faithful witness (Ps. 126:5-6).

Frequently, I have thought of that memorable scene in the award-winning movie, *Chariots of Fire,* when British track star Eric Liddell explained to his sister, Jenny, why he must run in the 1924 Paris Olympics, delaying his departure to the mission field in China. "God made me fast," said Eric, "and when I run I feel His pleasure." In much the same way as we serve the Lord—not in our strength, but by His Spirit—we feel His joy (Psalms 86:4). We are doing what He created, redeemed, and gifted us to do. His joy and His pleasure are our strength. We have "food" the world knows nothing about, and the longer we serve Him and the longer we fellowship with Him, the greater becomes that joy. Modern-day disciples can relate the experience of Jesus' disciples at the wedding in Cana. When He is the invited guest, He transforms water into wine and saves "the best til now" (John 2:10). *Every day* with Jesus may not seem "sweeter than the day before," but His presence produces new delights!

The Christian also lives in anticipation of an infinite degree of joy of which all present joys are but a foretaste. All the faithful people of God have been sustained through life's trials by the confident expectation of "better and lasting possessions" (Heb. 10:34) and of that day of passing from this mortal life of partial joy into the everlasting life of being "overjoyed when His glory is revealed" (1 Pet. 4:13). This anticipation of "the joy set before Him" sustained our Lord Jesus Christ in his arduous journey to the cross (Heb. 12:2).

The joy within us is the joy of His presence, power, and purpose. The joy before us is the joy of His fullness of glory which He will share with us. We will know His unmitigated, unbroken fellowship. We will know His full pleasure that finally we have reached the goal of accomplishing His purpose of godliness, and of reflecting His glory on earth (Rom. 8:20, Ezek. 36:23).

To be holy as He is holy is to share this heavenly joy the world cannot understand. Sangster related an experience that pictures in bold relief the contrast between the world's unholy attempt to enjoy itself and the Christian's blissful enjoyment of God.

"I stood outside a church one Sunday evening and watched the worshippers disperse. God had come very near to His people that evening. The awful hush of His presence was on them as they turned to walk quietly home.

"A crowded motor coach, returning with revellers from the seaside, was checked by the traffic for a minute. The occupants were flushed with too much drink; they were wearing paper caps and false noses and singing scraps of comic songs.

"For some reason, the dispersing worshippers appeared amusing to them. They flung streamers of coloured paper over the people leaving church, and one bibulous passenger called out: 'Why don't you enjoy yourself?'

"Two ways of life had met for an instant. The coach rolled on with that question hanging on the air: 'Why don't you enjoy yourself?' It is those who think they are artists in enjoying themselves who so signally fail; whose enjoyment leaves a 'hangover' . . .

"Bliss is the prerogative of the saint."[4]

Notes

1. C. S. Lewis, *Surprised by Joy* (London: Collins, 1955).

2. For a full discussion of the relationship between joy and spiritual discipline, see Calvin Miller, *The Taste of Joy* (Downers Grove, Ill.: InterVarsity Press, 1983).

3. Brother Lawrence, *The Practice of the Presence of God* (Old Tappan N.J.: Fleming H. Revell Co., 1958).

4. W. E. Sangster, *The Pure in Heart* (London: The Epworth Press, 1954), p. 112.

4

Holiness Is Peace

. . . the fruit of the Spirit is *peace* . . . (Galatians 5:22).

Rejoice in the Lord always. I will say it again: Rejoice! Let your gentleness be evident to all. The Lord is near. Do not be anxious about anything, but in everything, by prayer and petition, with thanksgiving, present your requests to God. And the peace of God, which transcends all understanding, will guard your hearts and your minds in Christ Jesus (Philippians 4:4-7).

Peace I leave with you; my peace I give you. I do not give to you as the world gives. Do not let your hearts be troubled and do not be afraid (John 14:27).

Holiness includes the attribute of peace. As we grow in holiness, through our lives of obedient dependence upon the indwelling Spirit of holiness, we will be strengthened by these Christlike attributes Paul described as the fruit of the Spirit. We have considered love, the first attribute listed, and have noted that love is the dominant and key aspect of the fruit of the Spirit. We noted from passages like 1 Corinthians 13 that if *agapē* love abounds in us, we will develop these other aspects of the fruit of the Spirit. Yet, we need to understand each aspect of the fruit of the Spirit in order to understand the nature of holiness, which we are to pursue if we are to see the Lord (Heb. 12:14).

In the previous chapter we considered joy as part of this cluster of the fruit of the Spirit. Holiness involves joy which comes from our trust relationship with Christ, a joy that is lasting, indomita-

ble, and not dictated by our circumstances of our world, our sur-
roundings, and even of our personal lives. I will not have to con-
vince you of the absence of peace on the current international
scene. Peace-keeping efforts, such as in the Middle East, are par-
tially or temporarily successful at best. International and intrana-
tional conflicts aside, we recognize the absence of peace in
practically every kind of human relationship. Increasingly, we
hear police reports that one of the most violent battlegrounds is
the American home, where physical abuse often characterizes hus-
band-wife and parent-child relationships.

Even if the globe were to come under a world government such
as George Orwell predicted in his classic *1984,* and by a world
military force all uprisings were to fall under some type of control,
such would not present peace in the true sense of the word. Should
we be able to find sufficient personnel to place an armed guard in
every home, school, and tavern in America, this would not insure
genuine peace.

Peace in the biblical sense is far more than the absence of conflict. The Old Testament word for peace, *shalom,* means the
strength and completeness of our sense of well-being that comes
from our relationship with God. Peace is not merely freedom from
trouble, but rather "everything that makes for a man's highest and
best good."[1] Through a personal experience with God's love, forgiveness, and presence in our lives, we have a new sense of well-
being that brings us spiritual wholeness and health.

The New Testament word for peace is *eirēne,* this inner spiritual
well-being that comes with our new nature in Christ, and grows
as a vital part of the developing fruit of the Spirit.

The World's Peace

Perhaps the place to begin in understanding this peace is to
determine what it is not. It is not the world's concept of peace.
Jesus said to His disciples, who faced the imminent suffering and
persecution that would accompany their mission in a hostile

world, "Peace I leave with you; My peace I give you. I do not give to you as the world gives" (John 14:27). Even as the unbelieving world has its definitions for love and joy, so also for peace. Many in the world would say the only real and attainable peace is on the international, political level. Though we as Christian citizens of this globe and peace-loving nation must pray and work toward political peace, yet we know the Lord's prophecy that there would continue to be, until His second coming, wars and rumors of wars. Wars are essential acts of aggression between hateful, greedy, fearful, and desperate societies and their leaders.

Some who have despaired of constructing a peaceful society have withdrawn into communes and cults that promise a peaceful utopia. Many if not most of these have degenerated into places of internal strife and conflict. Even the church, throughout its history, has experimented with peace by withdrawal from the world's conflicts. The Roman Catholics had their golden age of monasticism which, tellingly enough, took place during the Dark Ages of Western Civilization. Evangelicals like us tend to, in the name of peace, withdraw from involvement in the world.

Yet, Jesus came not to bring peace to the status quo, but the sword of challenge, division, and conflict. The peace He promised to His followers was peace with God and with others in His Kingdom army, and peace within the forgiven self, but we are to go into the battle against Satan and his forces (Matthew 10:34). We will endure opposition and persecution and will have trouble in the world, Jesus said, but "in me you may have peace," and He has overcome the world (John 16:33).

The world seeks peace politically by idealistic activism or by complacency with the status quo. The world seeks peace in relationships by trying to intimidate the opposition (e.g., violence in the home, spouse and child abuse), or by running from conflict (e.g., parental absenteeism, marital separation, and rampant, easy divorce). The world may seek personal peace by trips into bizarre meditation exercises, psychotherapies, and experimentation with and/or indulgence in drugs and alcohol. Others may not trip out on drugs, but withdraw from life's involvement by becoming secretive, reclusive, and terribly self-centered. The world's peace is based on either the unlikely absence of war and strife, the elusive tranquility of circumstances, or the escape of pain through artificial and temporary trips on drugs, alcohol, or hedonistic pleasures.

The Christian's peace, however, is absolute and permanent, unchanged by the circumstances of life. It is the peace seen in the face of Stephen as he witnessed prior to his martyrdom (Acts 6:15). It is the peace in the heart of Paul as he encouraged the others on board the storm-tossed ship (Acts 27:25). It is the peace of Jesus who could give Himself over to those who would crucify Him, knowing His Father was in absolute control of the circumstances (John 18:4*ff*).

God's Peace

Jesus promised us the gift of His unique peace, unlike anything the world can give (John 14:27). "A great company of the heavenly host" joined the angel, who had announced to the shepherds the birth of the Christ child, and shouted in praise, "Glory to God in the highest, and on earth peace to men on whom his favor rests" (Luke 2:14). The Incarnation of the Son of God presented the possibility of peace to mankind, alienated from God and distressed by the guiltiness of unforgiven sin. Long before Isaiah the prophet described this inveterate restlessness of sinful, rebellious man:

> But the wicked are like the tossing sea, which cannot rest, whose waves cast up mire and mud. "There is no peace," says my God, "for the wicked." (Isa. 57:22*ff*).

The birth of the Savior, however, signaled God's initiative in bringing peace with God, the basis for peace with oneself and others.

This peace with God came at a great price. The combined cost of all the world and civil wars of the ages fought to settle the disputes of nations pales in comparison with the price God paid for our peace. Because of our willful sin, we had become God's enemies, the objects of His holy wrath. Because of this dreadful clash of wills between a holy God and sinful mankind, someone had to initiate peacemaking, i.e., reconciliation. In the Christ Event (incarnation, atonement, and resurrection) this holy God demonstrated His infinite love and mercy by reconciling the world unto Himself (2 Cor. 5:19).

We who were alienated from God and "enemies in (our) minds because of (our) evil behavior" have been reconciled "by Christ's physical body through death" (Col. 1:21-22). We "rejoice in God through our Lord Jesus Christ, through whom we have now received reconciliation" (Rom. 5:11). We who were the alienated objects of His wrath, upon our repentance of sin and acceptance of His gift, have become the recipients of His saving grace, love and friendship. We who were without hope and God in the world, who were once far away, have now in Christ "been brought near through the blood of Christ" (Eph. 2:13). What a price He paid for our peace!

More than that, Paul said, "he himself is our peace" (Eph. 2:14). He doesn't invest in us an outside property called peace, He Himself comes to reside in us through the Holy Spirit. And the Holy Spirit makes desirable, essential, and possible our peace with one another. We who have received God's forgiveness through Christ now forgive and find forgiveness from all fellow believers who are living in His peace, built into His holy temple of peace (Eph. 2:14-22).

Even as the peace of God was procured at a great price, so this divine gift is described as great peace, far surpassing what we can negotiate or fabricate (Pss. 37:11; 119:165). The indwelling Christ, who enters our lives at the moment of rebirth, is the perfect Peacemaker and Peacekeeper. We experience the peace of His acquittal for the guilt of all sin—past, present, and future. This is the peace that comes with justification, our being made right with God once-for-all. But also the God of peace gives the constant and even progressive peace that comes with sanctification, our growth in holiness and wholeness. "May God himself," prayed Paul the apostle, "the God of peace, sanctify you through and through" (1 Thess. 5:23). Our peace with God is more than the absence of conflict with a guilty conscience. We are indwelt with the Prince of peace whose will is to create in us all the properties that make for holiness and wholeness. As we become more like Christ, more graced with the whole fruit of the Spirit, we have a peace that the world and even immature Christians know nothing about.

This peace with God, maintained by fellowship with the One we love and seek to obey, is both internal and indestructible. This peace, unlike the world's peace, does not depend on outward circumstances or even presence of enemies or absence of friends.

Jesus warned us that our alliance with Him would evoke opposition and even persecution from unsuspected quarters, including perhaps even our own families (Matt. 10:34-36). Because we follow and imitate Him, we can expect Satan and the world under his influence to treat us in ways similar to what Jesus endured (John 15:18-25). But even severe outward assaults cannot disturb our inner peace we have in Christ.

> I have told you these things, so that in me you may have peace. In this world you will have trouble. But take heart! I have overcome the world. (John 16:33).

We know the One who is our peace will never leave or forsake us, though others and peaceful conditions may. The Word of God exhorts us to rejoice in the Lord always, knowing the Lord is near. And then, knowing His nearness, we must not be anxious about anything,

> but in everything, by prayer and petition, with thanksgiving, present your requests to God. And the peace of God, which tran-

scends all understanding, will guard your hearts and your minds in
Christ Jesus (Phil. 4:4-7).

Paul described the peace of God as a sentry who vigilantly
guards our hearts and minds, warding off any anxious thoughts
that would threaten our well-being. God is always there to stand
guard, but only through the disciplines of rejoicing, praying, and
trusting can we enjoy His peace. Much like the child who has
forgotten his parents are nearby, is fearful of the dark, so we are
needlessly afraid of circumstances and people who are under the
watchful eye of the Heavenly Father. We are promised perfect
peace if our mind is steadfastly trusting in God, yet perhaps one
of the most difficult spiritual exercises is the practice of His nearness (Isa. 26:3).

This mindfulness of God that causes us to focus on the positive
rather than the negative—on the true, noble, right, pure, lovely,
admirable, and praiseworthy—is a mindset conditioned by the
systematic reading of, memorizing of, and meditation upon the
Word of God, and by a vital, regular prayer life which cultivates
a sense of the nearness and guidance of a loving Heavenly Father
(Phil. 4:8-9). Such a peace-inducing mindset will give no place to
thoughts that disturb our peace or distract us in our fellowship
with God. Our enemy, the devil, "prowls around like a roaring
lion" (1 Pet. 5:8), seeking to devour us with anxiety and fear, but
we are invited to humble ourselves under God's mighty hand of
protection and to cast all our anxiety on Him, knowing He cares
for us. The devil would assail our assurance of our salvation, but
we must remember that "the God of peace will soon crush Satan"
under our feet, and as the children of God we have the authority
to rebuke the accuser (Rom. 16:20).

There are times when even our own consciences (our hearts)
would condemn us, but God "is greater than our hearts," and by
His word and the indwelling Holy Spirit, God reassures us that we
are His children and the objects of His love and care (1 John

3:19-22). Our Lord Jesus Christ, who in His incarnation limited Himself to the nature of one absolutely dependent upon the Father, also taught us to trust in God's sovereign care and provision for our every need. The life fully surrendered to God's will and purpose has no need for anxiety over material provisions or protection from danger.

The trusting life does not preclude our responsibilities to work, save, care for ourselves, and provide for our families. But the follower of Jesus Christ has abandoned the anxious pursuit of material and financial autonomy, and views his or her life, possessions, and overall well-being as a means to serving and glorifying God, who will see that we have what we need for this higher purpose (Matthew 6:25-34). The oft-quoted verse, Romans 8:28 is not a promise of fortuitous circumstances and unbroken tranquility, but rather a robust reminder that the sovereign God whom we love and seek to serve is faithfully at work in all our circumstances for our spiritual good and His eternal glory. We can rest assured that He is moving us toward His desired destiny, our complete conformity to the likeness of His Son (Rom. 8:29). As faith gives us the bigger picture, we can be at peace even with our enemies.

Because he knew the gospel was being preached, Paul could with strong confidence accept his imprisonment and not be distressed that his enemies were causing him personal trouble (Phil. 1:12-18). Because he could by faith see the sovereign hand of God behind and beyond his immediate circumstances, Joseph was able to be patient during his years of adversity, and at peace with his brothers who had so grossly wronged him. "You intended me harm," he explained to his brothers, "but God intended it for good to accomplish what is now being done, the saving of many lives" (Gen. 50:20)

We too will begin enjoying the peace of God when we no longer seek first our personal peace and prosperity—but begin to love and serve God with a larger concern for the growth of His kingdom and a resultant confidence that He never sleeps but keeps vigilant guard over the steps of His servant-children (Ps. 121:3-4).

What a precious gift is this peace of God. I must admit my frequent failure to enjoy this peace, but with dependence upon the Holy Spirit, I must resolve to experience this important aspect of holiness. We must be holy because He is holy, and He is the God of peace (Rom. 16:20).

God's Peacemakers

The peace that is essential to holiness is not, however, exclusively personal. We must throughout our striving for holiness resist the temptation to be self-occupied. We must not overlook the benediction of being God's peacemakers, which includes being acclaimed as the sons of the God of all peace (Matt. 5:9). Obviously, the Christian participates in all endeavors for a peaceful society and world, in both prayer and support of peacemaking endeavors, regardless of the political channels the individual might deem most effective. We are to intercede for "all those in authority, that we might live peaceful and quiet lives in all godliness and holiness" (1 Tim. 2:1-2). The personal pursuit of holiness is certainly enhanced by a well-ordered society made possible by the exercise of proper civil and military authority which God has established to protect society from criminal domestic and international behavior (Rom. 13:1-7).

Even as the biblical concept of peace transcends merely the absence of conflict, even so our task of peacemaking demands more than responsible citizenship. Even higher than the demand to "give to Caesar what is Caesar's" is our responsibility to give to God what is God's including our efforts to enhance His peace in the lives of His people and the life of His church (Matt. 22:21).

Christ has indeed called us to peace and to be at peace with one another, but because Christians sometimes resort to conduct characteristic of the old unconverted life:

the acts of the sinful nature are . . . hatred, discord, jealousy, fits
of rage, selfish ambition, dissensions, factions and envy . . . (Galatians 5:19*ff*),

measures must be taken by God's peacemakers to protect the unity
of the church. Paul used his apostolic authority to challenge the
Corinthian Church to exercise discipline against individuals and
groups that threatened the unity of the church. He directed the
Roman believers to watch out for those who cause divisions (Rom.
16:17) and advised Titus to warn a divisive person once or twice,
but then after that "have nothing to do with him" (Titus 3:10).

Obviously, the peaceful fellowship of the church was a high
priority to the apostle Paul, but also to our Lord Himself. In His
Sermon on the Mount, Jesus commanded us to seek peaceful
reconciliation to our offended brother before we could worship
(Matt. 5:12*ff*). Even if we are offended ones, we are to go to the
offender, following our Lord's directive for the discipline and protection of church fellowship (Matt. 18:15-20). In our impersonal,
free-spirited society even we who are in the great counterculture,
the church, are likely to disregard the necessity for peaceful relationships. Because we have for so long disregarded much of church
discipline, should we begin enforcing these New Testament requirements, we would hardly know where to begin.

Yet, because our Lord has designed that the world would know
we are His disciples by our love for one another, we must take
seriously our calling to be His peacemakers with His body, the
church (John 13:35). We need also to recognize that our peace with
God and with one another is precious enough to be purchased by
the blood of Christ, whose death on the cross made possible our
dropping all hostilities and embracing one another as "members of
God's household" (Eph. 2:19). Our peace is His gift to us, but
because we don't always embrace and enjoy His gifts of peace we
must be reminded of our responsibility to "make every effort to
keep the unity of the Spirit through the bond of peace" (Eph. 4:3).

We are God's peacemakers, not by asserting our rights and seeking to manipulate others, but rather by being submissive in spirit. Being filled with the Holy Spirit, having the serving, humble mindset of our Lord Jesus, we can then "submit to one another out of reverence for Christ" (Eph. 5:21). It's past time for those of us in the church to realize who the real enemy is, and instead of attacking one another, begin to love and encourage one another in the battle against the world, the flesh, and the devil.

We who have been reconciled to God have been given the ministry of reconciliation. We who have peace with God must accept our responsibility to relate, by the witness of our lives and words, the way others can know the peace of God through faith in Jesus Christ. We represent the Prince of peace in a world resounding with hostilities. Whenever we influence another life to come to peace terms with God through faith in Jesus Christ, we are serving the cause of peace on earth (2 Cor. 5:11-20). The Christian evangelist is God's peacemaker.

Holiness includes peace—with God and from God—the sense of well-being and completeness we have in our personal relationship with Him. This peace of God that transcends all understanding guards our hearts and minds in Christ Jesus, but also enriches relationships in the household of faith, and enables otherwise-hostile factions and to be at peace with each other. When we share the attributes of the One who is perfectly holy, we not only experience this peace, but we will relinquish personal ease and risk our own outward tranquility to pray and strive until "all the lands are at rest and at peace" (Isa. 14:7).

Note

1. William Barclay, *The Letter to the Galatians and Ephesians* (Philadelphia: The Westminster Press, 1958), p. 55.

5

Holiness Is Patience

. . . the fruit of the Spirit is . . . *patience* (Gal. 5:22)

Consider it pure joy, my brothers, whenever you face trials of many kinds, because you know that the testing of your faith develops perseverance (Jas. 1:2-3).

A man's wisdom gives him patience; it is to his glory to overlook an offense (Prov. 19:11).

Just prior to my move to another pastorate years ago, a member of the congregation I was leaving gave me a coffee mug imprinted with this prayer: "Lord, grant me patience, but hurry!" Although she may have misconstrued the reason for that resignation, yet she may have detected my genuine need for this very vital aspect of holiness.

The King James translation of the Greek *makrothumia* is the more descriptive word long-suffering. The dictionary definition of patience is quite comprehensive and biblical, stating that patience is "the capacity, habit, or fact of (1) bearing pains or trials calmly or without complaint; (2) manifesting forbearance under provocation or strain; (3) being steadfast despite opposition, difficulty or adversity; (4) being able or willing to bear."[1]

Perhaps no other virtue of holiness seems further from the reach of those of us who are born and bred in a day that expects quick service and instant results. Yet, our well-being and the effectiveness of our life and service seem dependent on this quality. Even

Even the most impatient of us can take heart. He who is holy and patient commands us to be holy and therefore patient. What God commands, He enables.

The Patience of God

In the Old Testament the Lord (*Yahweh*) is revealed as the God who called Israel to be the people of His covenant, to receive His promised blessings on the basis of His mercy, but also conditional upon Israel's obedience. You are familiar with the quite inglorious history of Israel's unfaithfulness and rebellion, yet also how God remained steadfast in His commitment to His people. This steadfastness is God's patience.

After the rebellion with the golden calf, when Moses smashed the tablets containing the Ten Commandments, God's judgment fell, but God did not give up on Israel. He, in patience, stayed with them.

> He passed in front of Moses, proclaiming . . . "And he passed in front of Moses, proclaiming, "The Lord, the Lord, the compassionate and gracious God, slow to anger, abounding in love and faithfulness, maintaining love to thousands, and forgiving wickedness, rebellion and sin" (Ex. 34:6-7a).

Following the rebellion of the Israelites who refused to believe the good report of Joshua and Caleb, the Lord declared to Moses that "the Lord is slow to anger, abounding in love and forgiving sin and rebellion" (Num. 14:18a).

Over and over again, we see God is not capricious, but even His wrath against sinners is always under control. He punishes but never unjustly, and He always extends mercy and grace until His wrath is His last resort. Unlike man, who often is short-tempered and quick to react, and unlike the capricious gods of the Canaanites whose wrath had to be appeased, God is a patient, long-tempered God whose desire is to bless, not to destroy.

The God of the New Testament is exactly the same as the God

of the Old Testament, but in Jesus Christ, the Son of God, we have a fuller, more graphic revelation of God. In Jesus we view the perfect patience of God. He demonstrated His patience as long-suffering and tolerance toward the often disappointing disciples, who were slow of heart to believe and obey. He quietly endured the pain of His unjust and seemingly unbearable circumstances, which were necessarily endured for the sake of our salvation (Heb. 5:8-10). Jesus persevered and remained steadfastly patient, even in His death on the cross (Heb. 12:2). Also, the Savior revealed infinite patience toward sinners, and sought patiently to bring them to Himself in saving grace. He came, continually seeking the lost, (Luke 19:10), and inviting them to His salvation rest, (Matt. 11:28-30).

Paul wrote that God is justified in His wrath toward sinners, and that His judgment is inescapable. But also God's patience in withholding His stored-up wrath is calculated to lead sinners toward repentance (Rom. 2:1-5). Peter wrote that "God waited patiently in the days of Noah," delaying His judgment (1 Pet. 3:20), but also that God continues in patience "not wanting anyone to perish, but everyone to come to repentance" (2 Pet. 3:9).

God is perfectly patient, tolerant, and long-suffering of us (even when He is justified in immediate punishment/destruction). God in Christ, has provided for our salvation and forgiveness, and is patient until His elect be gathered in. But also, once we become His children, He continues to be patient in our spiritual development.

The Patience of Believers

The patience of God is part of His holy character. We are called to share in His full holiness, and if we would be obedient and fulfill our calling, we too will become patient. We will urgently *pursue* patience as we quietly wait on God to grant it in His way.

If I were to attempt a definition of patience that would "Christianize" the dictionary, I would say "patience is the Spirit-controlled reaction to pains, trials, disappointments, or irritations that come through circumstances or persons, including myself." We must remember that the Christian's key to spiritual success, in holiness or service, is the presence and power of the Holy Spirit, but the acquiring of these Spirit-inspired qualities is *our* responsibility. We must determine to seek and find these God-provided characteristics. We must recognize our *need* for patience. Your friend or spouse may recognize it, but do *you* recognize your need for patience?

To be long-tempered instead of short-tempered, to be tolerant of others and their irritations, and then, to learn to wait upon the Lord. To be steadfast in service even when the spiritual and emotional support seems to be lacking, when God is silent. To stand steadfast with endurance when burdens and trials keep coming, and pain keeps wracking your body and distracting your mind; to keep on persevering in good works when others don't notice or appreciate you, when success is eluding you, or perhaps others are opposing you.

Patience, perhaps more than any other attribute, reveals the real mettle of your Christian character. W. E. Sangster said there are many who are great Christians as long as things are going well, but when adversity comes, their Christian commitment seems to shrivel.[2] Only a cheap, "Hollywoodish" type gospel will tell you your problems are over when you become a Christian, that you will be rich, famous, and successful if you only have faith. The authentic gospel, however, tells you many of your problems just begin when you become a Christian. The believer sees his or her new problems as opportunities to grow in character described as holy, which includes this important attribute of patience.

The Development of Patience

God does grant patience with our cooperation. First, in thinking of the development of patience, we must realize it is a grace gift, part of the fruit of the Spirit in our yielded, obedient, and receptive lives. The unbeliever can know nothing of God's patience and the grace of patience, and though he may have humanly acquired, stoical resilience, yet he could not begin to face the special adversity a Christian at times must face with true patience.

Though patience is a God-given grace, yet we must develop patience in *our* lives by our obedience and faith response to others and to circumstances. We must, first of all, remember the patience of God toward us and realize *our* responsibility to be patient. Jesus told the parable of the man forgiven the debt of several million dollars who was unwilling to forgive the man who owed him but a few dollars, and had him thrown into prison (Matt. 18:23-35). God was patient and long-tempered with us, and we must relate to others with the same tolerance.

I heard a preacher confess that he lost his temper in traffic and his little boy/passenger remarked, "Daddy, we'd be good Christians if we didn't have to drive, wouldn't we?" It's incredible the spiritual mountains we can soar and then jump in the car to travel a few miles and virtually lose our Christianity behind the wheel of our automobiles.

God knew *exactly* what I needed when He gave me my wife! On our honeymoon, as we traveled eastward to travel the Skyline Drive through Virginia, I was irritated by the driver ahead who slowed down indecisively and pulled over onto the shoulder of the entry ramp, and then began backing up to get back onto the main highway. As I swerved around him, I muttered, "What's that idiot doing!" As I drove a bit farther, I realized I made the wrong turn, was getting onto the wrong turnpike. I didn't know what to do, and asked, "Nancy, what should I do?" She cattily replied, "Just back up and do what that *other* idiot did."

I think I have discovered perhaps the basis of that kind of temper and intolerance of other's mistakes. It's the problem of pride that says, "I'm so nearly perfect, why can't others be more like me? Why can't others be perfect drivers, or perfect employees, or perfect Christians and church members?" Was not spiritual pride the source of disunity in the early church?

Paul admonished the Ephesians to "be completely humble" . . .

> As a prisoner for the Lord, then, I urge you to live a life worthy of the calling you have received. Be completely humble and gentle; be patient, bearing with one another in love. Make every effort to keep the unity of the Spirit through the bond of peace (Eph. 4:1-3).

He advised the Colossians to "clothe yourselves with compassion . . .

> Therefore, as God's chosen people, holy and dearly loved, clothe yourselves with compassion, kindness, humility, gentleness, and patience. Bear with each other and forgive whatever grievances you may have against one another. Forgive as the Lord forgave you. And over all these virtues put on love, which binds them all together in perfect unity (Col. 3:12-14).

We need to exercise the grace of patience that says God has accepted me and forgives me of my sins and imperfections, which are many, therefore, to preserve unity, I must accept others and encourage them, remembering God is not through working with any of us yet. We're all spiritual "kids under construction."[3]

We are also responsible to grow in patience toward our circumstances, to react with endurance, to stand up under trials and heavy burdens. Paul said,

> we also rejoice in our sufferings, because we know that suffering produces perseverance; perseverance, character; and character, hope. And hope does not disappoint us, because God has poured out his love into our hearts by the Holy Spirit, whom He has given us (Rom. 5:3-5).

James wrote that we are to

> Consider it pure joy, my brothers, whenever you face trials of many

kinds, because you know that the testing of your faith develops perseverance. Perseverance must finish its work so that you may be mature and complete, not lacking anything" (Jas. 1:2-4).

Not one of us with purely human reaction could savor trials, be they illness, pain, financial loss, or severe disappointment. But the Christian comes to understand, sometimes during adversity, that God is more interested in our spiritual development than in our immediate pleasure. God has the longer view. He has our eternal interests at heart. He allows adversity and disappointment, and at times seems to be silent, to leave us all alone in our days, weeks, perhaps years of waiting and struggling, in order to wean us from the world and produce in us a character otherwise impossible. Even Jesus Himself became complete and learned obedience through the things He suffered.

Joseph's character and ability to lead Egypt in their time of crises and to preserve his brothers, the heads of the tribes of Israel, were developed in those years he languished in prison, seemingly forgotten by man and God. Joseph had patience, however, and could keep himself under God's control because he had an indomitable conviction of the sovereignty of God (Gen. 50:20).

We must learn to react to circumstances that might include opposition or even overt persecution in such a way as to develop perseverance in service. We stand with endurance, but we go *forward* with perseverance. Keep on being obedient in character, keep on serving God even when it's difficult, costly, and unrewarding to do so. We have been given great biblical examples of those who patiently endured suffering and persevered in their service (Heb. 6:12 and Jas. 5:10). Like Jesus, they could foresee the glory before them, and realized this world was not their final home (Heb. 12:2).

It takes *time* to develop patience—thus the absurdity of the prayer, "God grant me patience, but hurry!" The best sprinter in the world is more than likely a poor long-distance runner. We need the patience of the long view. We are training for eternity. God can be patient and long-tempered because He is eternal, He can see the long view, the outcome. He can scan all of eternity with the blink of His eye. He knows that lost husband will be saved, those prayers of the heartbroken wife will be answered. God knows that your flawed character will ultimately become perfect some day.

The unsaved need to view God's patience as His kindness that leads to repentance (Rom. 2:4). Other Christians need to repent of our impatience, our intolerance, and our complaining, distrustful attitudes toward our circumstances and others. We need to ask for the grace to consider our trials pure joy! Then, indeed, greater will be our holiness.

Notes

1. *Webster's Ninth New Collegiate Dictionary* (Springfield, Mass.: G. & C. Merriam Co., 1983).

2. W. E. Sangster, *The Pure in Heart* (London: The Epworth Press, 1954), p. 125.

3. Bill & Gloria Gaither, Ron Huff & Joy MacKenzie, Title of Children's Musical, *Kids Under Construction: A Musical Blueprint for Becoming* (Alexandria, Ind.: Gaither Music Co., 1981).

6

Holiness Is Kindness and Goodness

> . . . the fruit of the spirit is . . . *kindness, goodness* . . . (Gal. 5:22, NIV).
>
> . . . add to your faith . . . brotherly kindness . . . (2 Pet. 1:15).

Kindness and goodness are two aspects of the fruit of the Spirit that are closely related, and because of their complementary relationship, need to be considered together. The King James translation of the Greek word *chrestotes* is gentleness, but kindness is a better rendering. The concept of gentleness will appear later in our study. Kindness focuses on the inner disposition influenced by the Holy Spirit to be sensitive toward others and sincerely desirous of their well-being. I think it was E. Stanley Jones who said goodness is "kindness with its sleeves rolled up." Goodness is the active response to our kindness of thought and attitude. It is the righteousness of God at work in and through us in behalf of others. Kindness issues in goodness. Kind thoughts give birth to good works. As William Barclay said, goodness is a "wider word" than kindness, and includes the possibility of the use of discipline and correction for the purpose of someone's betterment![1]

Kindness

The Bible and Christian faith often radically redefine words such as love and kindness. The world will use "kindness" to refer to a sentimental or soft approach to life as a sort of panacea for all the world's ills. Some would espouse an attitude of leniency and moral compromise, all in the name of kindness. But just a glimpse at the Savior, who is our perfect example of holiness (and in particular, kindness) shows us that to be kind does not mean to be soft or sentimental. Jesus' zeal for righteousness stirred Him with anger as He overturned the tables of the money changers and drove them and their animals out of the temple courts.

The Apostle Paul's life was hardly soft or sentimental. He could warn the Corinthians of his anger and discipline, and when he gave an account of his hardships, he reminded them that through it all he had remained patient and kind (2 Cor. 6:3-6). The world sees kindness like a marshmallow—too soft and sweet for anyone's good.

The moral requirements of our Lord in the Sermon on the Mount and the characteristics of holiness that Paul expounded are applicable only to the Christian who is enabled to live in a righteousness that exceeds that of the scribes and Pharisees. This enablement is by grace, the power of the Holy Spirit, and a personal relationship with Jesus Christ. General society, on the other hand, must be governed by absolutes, that externally enforce conformity to social behavior. The unregenerate must be under the control of a society that has a pattern of law enforcement and punishment of the guilty. For example, it is absurd, in the name of kindness, for a society to allow violations of laws that are meant to protect others. I read of a lady juror who pursuaded her fellow jurors to decide for the innocence of a woman who had murdered her husband. "After all," she pleaded, "the poor woman is a widow!"[2] The kindness that is a vital part of our holiness is not social or moral leniency; nor does it indulge with leniency or indiscriminate tifts the lazy or rebellious. The kindest thing some parents could do for their spoiled children is to start exercising strong and wise discipline.

Holy kindness is not based on a sentimental God who indulges us. God, who loves us more than we could know, cares about our eternal spiritual good and sometimes denies us our wishes and allows us to experience difficulties, disappointments, and even His chastisement, which for the moment at least is not pleasant but produces holiness (Heb. 12:11). The Lord Jesus, the manifestation of God, is kind with sinners but harsh with sin. He with kindness forgave the woman taken in adultery whom the self-righteous, unkind religionists would have stoned to death. But also He told her to "go now and leave your life of sin" (John 8:3-11).

The kindness of God does not mean the cancellation of His wrath and final judgment. Paul said God's present kindness is meant to lead sinners to repentance before the release of His irrevocable wrath, being stored against them for the day of His wrath (Rom. 2:4-5). Jesus in kindness and compassion yearned for and lamented over Jerusalem, who refused to repent and faced imminent judgment (Luke 19:41-44).

Though kindness does not preclude judgment yet kindness is always presented as God's preference over judgment. His desire is that none perish, but all come to repentance, and Isaiah 28:21 notes that judgment is His "strange work," that which is a work of necessity (necessitated by His perfect justice), whereas kindness is His delightful attitude and forgiveness and grace His delightful work.

In the same way, we who are becoming holy as He is holy should not delight in telling sinners of God's judgment, but do so only because we must warn them. We should not delight in rebuking fellow believers, and if we must tell a painful truth it must be in love, with words seasoned with salt and carefully chosen. We must seek the fulness of the spirit of Christ, who could attract to Himself notorious, outcast sinners. He could engage the Samaritan woman in a dialogue that confronted her with truth, but truth spoken with kindness and love.

And Jesus was kind and considerate toward His own family, His disciples, and the multitudes. He provided for His mother, for wedding guests, and food for His disciples and the crowds. He was perfectly and always kind because He was totally selfless. He was the perfect servant who came not to be served, but to serve. We, on the other hand, often find kindness difficult because we are frequently self-serving and find others to be intrusions and obstacles in our way.

I mentioned that sinful pride is perhaps the nemesis of patience, and so it is with kindness. We have the impulse to become unkind when we think *our* schedule, *our* needs, *our* being treated with respect are of utmost importance. Often I am tested in the area of spiritual need which is the current subject in my sermon preparation! If I am to preach on patience I will find myself tested in such circumstances as hectic automobile traffic.

The week I studied the virtue of kindness I found myself tested by two store clerks and one waitress. I was tempted to say something unkind to three people who had the temerity to act as though my schedule were not the most important thing in the world! One overlooked me, another let someone else in line ahead of me. I was tempted to say something cutting and sarcastic, and probably did manage, even with the thin veneer of my ministerial demeanor, to communicate my displeasure. I have been so unkind on occassion to quite conceal my Christianity. Kindness in disposition, in voice, is perhaps our most frequently available opportunity to express the Spirit of Jesus to the general public. You can be kind to anybody in just about any amount of time.

We will share the kindness of Jesus as we remember the needs of others are more urgent than our own, and we are servants of Christ. We must realize that just as with our Lord, kindness should be our happy work, and leave judgment and vengeance to God, who reserves His judgment as His final work. We must be kind in our thoughts, attitudes, and words toward others, and make no provision for pride. Sometimes those who have won or are winning great spiritual battles and victories for God are unsympathetic with God's fallen, and want to shoot the wounded so they will not slow down the healthy troops. But we must realize our calling is to lift up the fallen; we are God's paramedics, His Florence Nightingales, and our purpose is to serve others to make *them* successful. Even as the Lord came to serve us, and stooped down to make us great (Ps. 18:35), so our usefulness and spiritual success in the eyes of God is measured by our being kindly disposed toward others. If there is kindness within, there can be goodness without.

Goodness

Goodness is kindness at work with its sleeves rolled up. "Kindness is a sincere desire for the happiness of others; goodness is the activity calculated to advance that happiness."[3] Goodness is the practical and sometimes costly follow-through expression of heartfelt kindness.

Just as kindness is epitomized in God, so is goodness. Job in his terrible ordeal and spiritual struggle did not answer to all his questions about suffering, but he did come to know God personally and realize His goodness (Job 42:5,10). The psalmist declared, "Give thanks to the Lord, for He is good. His love endures forever" (Ps. 136:1). God is Himself the standard for goodness, justice, and righteousness. He never violates His own moral law or His own goodness in any expression.

As James noted, when we are tempted we should not say, "God is tempting me: For God cannot be tempted by evil, nor does He tempt anyone" (Jas. 1:13). We are tempted and enticed by our own evil desire because God desires our righteousness. He does test the mettle of our faith and allows difficulties which may be part of His purpose to bring about our spiritual good (Rom. 8:28). God alone is perfectly good, and His Son Jesus reflects the perfect goodness of the Father (Luke 18:19).

Because of our fallen condition, the only way we can have righteousness acceptable to God is by faith in Jesus, and His righteousness/goodness is imputed to us. Now that we are saved by grace and acceptable to God through Christ, we are to grow in His practical, experiential righteousness that comes by our faith and obedience (Gal. 2:20). There must be a progressive death to sinful self that Christ's goodness might increasingly dominate our lives.

George Muller, the great man of holiness and faith, whose expansive orphanage ministry was a year-after-year series of the miracles of God's provision, was asked to give the secret of his great life and work. He reluctantly replied, "The day came when George Muller died to self!" Then, Muller had the grace to do good from a heart of compassion and kindness.[4]

Apart from grace our self-directed good works are in God's sight as "filthy rags" (Isa. 64:6). Sangster called the good works of the unregenerate as "Pharisaism in overalls," the attempt of those who reject God and godliness who try to prove their innate goodness by their acts of benevolence.[5] But God is not impressed.

Goodness, good works, or whatever the believer does as an expression of Christ's love and kindness in him or her, is the outworking of God's purpose. We often quote Ephesians 2:8-9, as the enunciation of the basis of our salvation, but we too often omit verse 10 which states the *purpose* of our salvation: "For we are God's workmanship, created in Christ Jesus to do good works, which God prepared in advance for us to do" (Eph. 2:10). When we do anything in behalf of another, to aid in a temporal or spiritual need, to contribute to the joy or success of another, we are following in the steps of Jesus who "went around doing good" (Acts 10:38).

We have noted the beautiful sequence in Jesus' ministry to the woman of Samaria. He reached out in His heart with kindness; His words were seasoned with kindness as He overcame the barriers of her resistance, and then He gave her the gift of His salvation as an act of doing her eternal good.

The good works God has prepared in advance for us to do may not all be great achievements (Eph. 2:10). This may include a phone call or visit of encouragement or good cheer to a lonely shut-in. Goodness often involves giving to the material needs of others, as did the Macedonians (2 Corinthians 8—9).

Goodness may be expressed through your daily vocation. Even assembly-line workers should be able to dedicate themselves to doing good for others and to do their best to help provide the best product for the good or enjoyment of others. God will put opportunities for doing good before us daily, sometimes in serendepitous ways. We will have opportunities for doing good in our daily relations in the church, the Body of Christ, and Paul said this is our prior responsibility.

If we don't provide the needs of our own immediate families (physical or spiritual) we are worse than unbelievers (1 Tim. 5:8). By the way, why is it our kindness most often fails within our own family relations? Is it because we don't feel social pressure to perform with our best behavior? Is it because we can vent our hostilities and negative emotions inside the secretive walls of our houses? Is it because we feel we can presume upon the good graces of our forgiving families and loved ones?

Paul includes the larger family of God as the realm of responsibility for goodness, saying, "as we have opportunity, let us do good to all people, *especially* to those who belong to the family of believers. How displeasing it is to God when we as brothers and sisters in Christ are *unkind* to each other and reluctant to do good deeds for each other. These are so crucial that Jesus, in His judgment passage, says good works done to His children will be the evidence to confirm our salvation! (Matt. 25:31*ff*). We are saved by grace, but just as outward evidence forms the basis for a jury's verdict and judge's sentence, so authentic grace has the certificate of definite acts of goodness. James said that faith without works is *dead,* and real, saving faith *works.*

Good works will not only be our evidence in the judgement, but are our evidence to the world that our gospel is real. Our good works are to be evident to the world and evidence that will bring the lost to sense the glory of God (Matt. 5:16). You may be discouraged and tired. The remedy is more good works because a harvest of good works will bring refreshment (Gal. 6:9).

Perhaps you are weary and saying to yourself, "I need some rest from serving God; let some of the younger folk or newer Christians do the work." Do I have a word for you! Paul said, "Let us not become weary in doing good." Then he gave the prescription for spiritual renewal and refreshment. Note, it is not in retreat or early retirement, but in persevering in doing good, saying, *"for at the proper time we will reap a harvest if we do not give up"* (Gal. 6:9).

The harvest brings the refreshment. Jesus was weary when He sat down at Jacob's well, yet He was not too weary to be kind to the woman who came to draw water.

Then, He did her good by His gift of living water and of His understanding and acceptance. When she discovered this great gift, she went back to Sychar with an excited witness about her newfound Savior.

This refreshed Jesus told His disciples He had been renewed by a food they didn't know anything about (John 4:32).

May we together seek after kindness and goodness, a vital part of holiness, without which we will not see the Lord (Heb. 12:14). We are saved by His grace to be holy, to be kind, and to do good. We know we someday will see the Lord because His nature in us enables us to be kind and to do good works that enable others to see Christ in us.

Notes

1. William Barclay, *The Letters to the Galatians & Ephesians* (Philadelphia: The Westminster Press, 1958), p. 56.

2. W. E. Sangster, *The Pure in Heart: A Study of Christian Sanctity* (London: The Epworth Press, 1954), p. 134

3. Jerry Bridges, *The Practice of Godliness* (Colorado Springs, Colo.: NavPress, 1983), p. 231.

4. W. E. Sangster, p. 141.

5. Ibid., p. 143

7

Holiness Is Faith/Faithfulness

. . . the fruit of the Spirit is . . . *faithfulness* (Gal. 5:22).

So then, just as you received Christ Jesus as Lord, continue to live in him, rooted and built up in him, strengthened in the faith as you were taught, and overflowing with thankfulness (Col. 2:6-7).

Many a man claims to have unfailing love, but a faithful man who can find? (Prov. 20:6).

The call to be holy is the call to faith and faithfulness. The Greek word *pistis* is (Gal. 5:22) translated "faith" in the King James Version and "faithfulness" in more recent translations. Though because of contextual reasons "faithfulness" is preferred, yet both are acceptable translations, and both concepts are vital ingredients in the life of holiness.

Already we have noted the distinct definitions our Christian faith gives to words used in everyday conversation. As in Christ we know love differently from the world, so with the word *faith.* People will have faith, generally speaking, in something or in someone. By this we mean they have an object of their confidence or trust. If they are adamantly distrustful of anything or anyone they will be found to have a trust in the principle that nothing or nobody is to be trusted! What makes faith a Christian ideal and a part of the fruit of the Spirit and the life of holiness is its object—Jesus Christ. Entrance into the kingdom of heaven is gained solely by our trust in God's gracious provision for our salvation through the death and resurrection of Jesus Christ (Rom. 3:22-26; 4:25). Salvation has no grounds for boasting in human works. It can be argued that not only God's grace but even our faith is a gift from God (Eph. 2:8-9).

Faithfulness, on the other hand, seems to have little place these days in the world's vocabulary, unless it is faithfulness to one's self. A self-centered age is basically an unfaithful age, and the evidence of the self-centeredness of our society abounds in the rampant divorce rate and in the wholesale abandonment of loyalties that have been traditionally important—loyalty to church, to country, to ethical values, to one's employer, and to family.

In stark contrast to the world's unfaithfulness is the believer's faithfulness both to God and to his fellow human beings. We who are becoming holy are necessarily becoming faithful. "Be holy, because I am holy" (1 Pet. 1:16b). This means we are to be faithful because God Himself is faithful.

The Faithfulness of God

In the Old Testament the Hebrew word *amān* describes the stability, firmness, and trustworthiness of God to remain unchanging in His divine character, to be firm and affirming of His promises and purposes for His people, and to be trustworthy in fulfilling His redeeming, loving plans and purposes for His people. The word *amēn* is closely related, and expresses the human response to God's faithfulness, saying "let it be." The *amēn,* as it were, affirms God's *amān.*[1]

The story of redemption is an account of the absolute faithfulness of God toward the people He had chosen to receive His covenant promises and the benefits of His steadfast love. God called Israel to be His unique people, and established a binding relationship based on His commitment to be their God, demanding their obedience to His Moral Law (e.g. Exodus 19—20). He gave signs and ceremonies (e.g. circumcision and passover) to remind them of this covenant relationship; throughout the history of Israel God remained faithful, though His people were frequently rebellious and generally faithless.

When Israel woefully disobeyed the covenant, even God's punishment was an expression of His faithfulness and desire to bring His people back to Himself. In the midst of his lament over the fall of the nation, Jeremiah had occasion for praise and thanksgiving.

> Because of the Lord's great love we are not consumed, for his compassions never fail. They are new every morning; great is your faithfulness (Lam. 3:22-23).

Now we who are included in God's new and eternal covenant, one written upon the hearts of our Spirit-born nature, established through the blood of the covenant, have greater reason to *amēn* the faithfulness of God (Heb. 9:12-15). As Paul wrote to Timothy, His faithfulness is irrevocable even when we lapse into momentary unfaithfulness (2 Tim. 2:13). We are eternally bound to the Savior who purchased our salvation with His own blood, the One who is "Faithful and True" (Rev. 19:11). Because He who called us is faithful, we must be faithful. But first, we must have faith.

Faith in God

Faith and faithfulness are important and vitally related aspects of holiness. Faithfulness is based upon and has its beginning in faith in God. Faith is the human response to the faithfulness of God. God was faithful to provide salvation, and the faith response is our receiving His provision. Not by works but by grace we are saved through faith (Eph. 2:8-9), and Paul developed in detail an exposition of Habakkuk 2:4 that states "the just shall live by faith" (Rom. 1:17).

The sinner's conscience is awakened, he or she repents of personal sin, and believes in Jesus as the Savior, calling upon Him to receive the gift of salvation. Paul upheld Abraham as an example for saving faith in that Abraham, despite the human evidence to the contrary, believed God, literally "He 'amēned' God," and God credited it to him as righteousness (Gen. 15:6; Rom. 4:3).

But now that we have received the gift of salvation, and are included in His eternal covenant, what happens to faith? We continue to trust God, to believe in Him and live by faith in His many promises to His children. Faith is exercised and expressed by obedience to God's Word and indwelling Spirit, who enables us to increasingly live by faith, not depending on human evidence (Heb. 11:1). For the Christian to continue to doubt God's word, and to seek external evidence and proof is a sign of spiritual immaturity and disobedience. Paul said,

> . . . just as you received Christ Jesus as Lord, continue to live in him, rooted and built up in him, strengthened in the faith as you were taught, and overflowing with thankfulness (Col. 2:6-7).

The Christian grows stronger in the faith that he or she practices at the moment of conversion, and the strengthening of faith does not come by focusing on faith, but focusing on God. As Tom Wright has expressed it, our faith may be small, but we have a great God.[2] Pagans often have strong faith in their superstitions and false gods, and quite often we Christians are put to shame by the faith and ardent faithfulness of pseudo-Christians and cult followers who devote years of servitude to the cause of their false religions.

We need to focus on our God who can do all things, and pray that we will not limit by our unbelief what He wants to do for us and through us. We ought to make our prayer the plea of the father of the demon-possessed boy, "Lord, I believe. Help me overcome my unbelief!" (Mark 9:24).

W. E. Sangster, who extensively studied the lives of godly people, noted that not many of the truly saintly people were exceptionally intelligent. He noted that oftentimes intelligence—or perhaps more accurately, intellectualism—becomes an impediment to faith. Intellectualism can distract with more reasons to question or doubt God, or lead one into the vain, futile search to understand mysteries that must ever remain mysteries till we see Jesus. This present life is meant to be lived, not unintelligently, but primarily by faith, by trusting God. Holiness is faith in God, but also is faithfulness to God and to others.

Faithfulness

The more we study and pursue holiness the more we realize the social dimension of the holy life. We are called to loving involvement and responsible relationships, including faithfulness to others. Holiness demands a tenacious loyalty and dependability the Bible calls faithfulness. God, who is the absolutely faithful One, expects and demands our loyalty to Him.

A liberating rediscovery in my spiritual and ministerial "identity crises" was to remember that my call to ministry was a call to stewardship.[3] What is required of stewards, those given a trust, is not a measurable level of ministerial performance with impressive results, but rather the proof of faithfulness (1 Cor. 4:2). I am accountable to God and the people I serve to faithfully discharge all the duties of my ministry (2 Tim. 4:5). If I am faithful, God will produce the fruit of visible results, but my focus is to be the faithful dispensation of my duties, and not the results.

Joseph was faithful to God, despite his often disheartening circumstances. He trusted God's sovereignty and loving purpose; he also was able to resist temptation because of his uncompromising loyalty to God, and was able to forgive his brothers because he knew God was in control (Gen. 50:20).

Daniel was faithful in his devotion to God. His enemies failed to find any flaw in his morals, and thus set him up for a choice between praying to God or obeying the king's edict. He was faithful to God and God delivered him (Dan. 6:22-23).

At the latter stage of his life, Paul could say, "I have fought the good fight, I have finished the race, I have kept the faith" (2 Tim. 4:7).

Hebrews 11 is the great roll call of the faithful, those who believed God against all odds and remained faithful witnesses unto death. Like Joseph, these heroes of faith and martyrs were steadfast even when the evidence of God's promises were absent (Heb. 11:39).

Anyone can be faithful to a sovereign who gives immediate rewards, but only those pursuing true holiness are faithful to God amidst all kinds of trials, the severest being the trial of faith that is described as "the dark night of the soul," when all spiritual comfort is gone.[4] The truly faithful will go on serving, praising, and trusting God when it is costly and apparently unrewarding.

Faithfulness to God demands faithfulness to others, just as loving God finds expression in loving one's neighbors. Faithfulness to others, and loyalty to others must be based upon our relationship to God. People, even the best of Christians, can be disappointing, and at times prove unworthy of our trust. Faithfulness, then, is evidence the Holy Spirit is at work in us. Demas, who proved unfaithful, fell in love with the world, which is basically unfaithful and self-serving (2 Tim. 4:10). But if we keep in mind that in serving them we are really serving God, who never disappoints, then we are never devastated. Disappointed, maybe, but never devastated (2 Cor. 4:8-9).

I think again of Joseph, who was betrayed by his brothers, falsely accused by Potiphar's wife, and forgotten by those he had befriended in prison. Yet, when God exonerated him, and he could have avenged himself on his brothers, he faithfully served them. His faithfulness to serving others was based on his trust in God, who meant everything for good (Gen. 50:20).

Barnabas was a great behind-the-scenes encourager whose faithfulness to others was based on his faithfulness to God. He believed in Paul's potential, and also in John Mark's who had forsaken him and Paul on the first missionary journey. Paul lost confidence, but Barnabas knew God was faithfully working on

John Mark. Paul later was forced to admit that Mark had become very useful to him (Acts 15:36-41; 2 Tim. 4:11).

There is no greater need in the Kingdom than for *faithfulness,* not only in pastors and church staff members, but in all the people of God. So many today church shop for what a church can offer them and soon become disillusioned or upset over the least offense, like a fastidious gourmet diner who vows never to return to a restaurant because they didn't serve him or her properly. We need to realize God is faithful to us, and called us to faithfully serve Him through His church.

God's kingdom doesn't want for talented people, but His churches need faithful people who are faithful to God's will for their lives in personal holiness, in relationships in the church, and in responsibility to the Great Commission. We are called to be faithful friends to one another, even in adversity. The world is full of "fair-weather" friends, but we need people in every church to be faithful to not only affirm each other, but even to rebuke one another, which is the caring, faithful response to a friend who is obviously out of the fellowship of God and His church. "The kisses of any enemy may be profuse, but faithful are the wounds of a friend" (Prov. 27:6). Christ Himself rebukes those He loves, and He admonishes us to do the same (Rev. 3:19, Luke 17:3).

We must be faithful to God and to His people. This we will do by the power of the Spirit and in the name of the One who is a Friend who "sticks closer than a brother" (Prov. 18:24). He is faithful to us. Let us be faithful to the One who is worthy of our complete trust and obedience.

Notes

1. E. C. Blackmun, "faith, faithfulness," E-J, *Interpreter's Dictionary of the Bible* (New York: Abingdon Press, 1962), pp. 222-234.

2. Tom Wright, *Small Faith, Great God: Biblical Faith for Today's Christians* (Old Tappan, N.J.: Fleming H. Revell Co., 1978).

3. John R. W. Stott, *The Preacher's Portrait: Some New Testament Word Studies* (Grand Rapids, Mich.: Wm. B. Eerdmans Co., 1961), pp. 11-32.

4. St. John of the Cross, *Dark Night of the Soul* (Garden City, N.Y.: Doubleday and Co., 1959)

8

Holiness Is Humility/Gentleness

... the fruit of the Spirit is ... *gentleness* (Gal. 5:22-23,).
Blessed are the meek, for they will inherit the earth (Matt. 5:5).
Come to me, all you who are weary and burdened, and I will give
you rest. Take my yoke upon you and learn from me, for I am gentle
and humble in heart, and you will find rest for your souls. For my
yoke is easy and my burden is light (Matt. 11:28-30).

We have already noted in our study of holiness, particularly in
examining the aspects of holiness Paul described as "the fruit of
the Spirit," that several of these biblical concepts are not easily
translated into our English language. Some of these one-word
characteristics of holiness have no one-English-word equivalent.
Also, we have seen that the closest English equivalent quite often
means something essentially different from the biblical concept.

The life of faith to a degree has its own vocabulary, just as it
has its own value system. We are of the kingdom of God and of
the Day, and the world and the darkness of Satan's kingdom of
unbelief does not, indeed cannot, understand or appreciate what
we know and love. This is particularly true in the realm of holiness. We believers know God personally through His saving grace,
and are now under His authority. He has commanded us to be holy
because He is holy and to share His nature. Through salvation He
has given to us "everything we need for life and godliness" (2 Pet.
1:3a), including a desire to be like Him in all holiness.

But we must take responsibility for our growth in holiness, and this we do by our study of holiness and our resolve, by God's grace, to conform our lives to these standards. As we study holiness, and the fruit of the Spirit, we are discovering what Jesus is like and what the Holy Spirit will enable us to become.

Our calling to be holy is a call to be *gentle* as God is gentle. The Greek word *praotes* means "meekness," or humility, as the King James Version translates it, but also means "gentleness." "Humility" carries a more active connotation, and describes our active submission to others, and "gentleness" speaks of our kind response to other people. Humility is placing ourselves at the mercy of others, and gentleness is our being kind, considerate, and gentle toward those who are at *our* mercy!

This characteristic of humility and gentleness, which should be the desire of all of us, is foreign to and even hated by the world apart from Christ.

Humility and Gentleness in the World

The mindset of the Greek and Roman world was expressed by Aristotle who declared that pride and high-mindedness were the best of virtues, and to be meek was to be weak.[1] Our society exalts the "macho" image of the brash and aggressive daredevil who walks along "muscle beach" kicking sand into the face of all the ninety-pound weaklings. Our society associates meekness with weakness, as we describe the timid little fellow as being "meek as a mouse."

Meekness, humility, and perhaps even gentleness are not in vogue today. To be a gentleman is hardly more than a polite designation or appellation, and the virtues of gentlemanliness are hardly espoused as once they were. These days I'm almost afraid to hold the door open for someone for fear my consideration will be interpreted as condescending patronage.

Today, humility and gentleness connote in some minds weakness, softness, or even effeminency. With some, these concepts conjure up thoughts of self-effacement and self-deprecation. To me it is not true humility, but rather artificial, pseudo-humility for someone to be always saying, "I'm no good, I'll never amount to anything." Such people, like the invalid at the pool of Bethesda, have grown dependent on and comfortable with their incapacity and have lost the will to succeed (John 5:1-15). Their so-called humility is an excuse for laziness—lack of basic ambition and drive—and is their license for being parasites on others.

Still others associate humility or gentleness with cowardice or passivity. There is a pacifism that is based on strong religious conviction which may be held by people of integrity and courage, but cowards will buy peace at any price, and will cower under the least intimidation. The world may call these despicable characteristics "humility" and/or "gentleness," but the biblical understanding of these words have an entirely different meaning.

The famed nineteenth-century British prime minister and statesman, William Gladstone, said "humility as a sovereign grace is the creation of Christianity," and I believe he was right.[2] Our Lord Jesus radically redefined humility and gentleness.

The Humility and Gentleness of Christ

Because humility carries the active connotation of submitting oneself before others, God the Father the Almighty One cannot be humble. He is to receive the submission and adulation of *all* His creation. But in the Incarnation of the Eternal Son, He has shown us perfect humility. Perhaps the greatest passage describing the humility of Christ is Philippians 2:1-11. Paul exhorted believers to "in humility consider others better than yourselves" and to look "to the interests of others." He then exhorted our imitation of the humility of Christ as expressed in the great Pleroma Hymn:

> Your attitude should be the same as that of Jesus Christ: Who, being in very nature God, did not consider equality with God something to be grasped, but made himself nothing, taking the very nature of

a servant, being made in human likeness. And being found in appearance as a man, he humbled himself and became obedient to death—even death on a cross! Therefore God exalted him to the highest place and gave him the name that is above every name, that at the name of Jesus every knee should bow, in heaven and on earth and under the earth, and every tongue confess that Jesus Christ is Lord, to the glory of God the Father" (Phil. 2:5-11).

God the Son humbled Himself and became dependent upon and obedient to God the Father. Taking on Himself the very nature of a servant "he humbled himself and became obedient to death—even death on a cross!" (verses 7—8). In His sacrificial, substitutionary death, Jesus glorified the Father by serving people, providing a ransom sacrifice for us. His was the servanthood in washing the disciples' feet (John 13:1-17).

As did Simon Peter, we might at first balk at the idea of the Son of God being our servant, but as Jesus told Simon Peter, unless we allow Him to be our servant, we have no part with Him (John 13:8). Because of Jesus' humbling Himself to do God's will and to serve us by dying for us, we have a share in God's eternal salvation. As we respond to God's salvation, by humbling ourselves in repentance of sin and trust in Jesus as Savior, we then experience His gentleness, which is His kind and acceptance response to our submission to Him (John 6:37).

God Almighty, God the Father, though He need not humble Himself, is gentle with those who come to Him. All of creation someday must bow before the Almighty and acknowledge that Jesus is Lord (Phil. 2:9-11). Those of us who have humbled ourselves at His feet in repentance and are trusting His grace and mercy have discovered His gentleness. Only those who refuse now to receive Jesus as Lord and Savior will meet His wrath and final rejection.

God Himself shows that gentleness does not preclude strength. Isaiah 40 describes the Almightiness of God (verses 10, 15, 2-26), but also says that He is a gentle Shepherd to His people.

> He tends his flock like a shepherd:
> he gathers the lambs in his arms
> and carries them close to his heart;
> he gently leads those that have young (Isa. 40:11).

Jesus, the Good Shepherd, revealed in human form the compatibility of strength with humility and gentleness. Jesus, in humility depended on the Father, and He obeyed the Father by serving mankind. His cleansing the temple, both at the beginning and ending of His earthly ministry, revealed His holy anger and forceful, even terrifying, capacity as "the Righteous Judge" (John 2:12-17; Luke 19:45-46).

But His desire is to be gentle and merciful, and invites us with

> Come to me, all you who are weary and burdened, and I will give
> you rest. Take my yoke upon you and learn from me, for I am gentle
> and humble in heart, and you will find rest for your souls. For my
> yoke is easy and my burden is light (Matt. 11:28-30).

He does not wish to destroy because our lives are already wrecked by sin (Matt. 12:20). Rather, He wishes to give us His rest and allow us to share in His victory (Matt. 11:29; 12:20-21). God is gentle. Jesus is humble and gentle. "Be holy because I am holy," God commands. By His grace and through our obedience we can also be holy and gentle.

The Humility and Gentleness of the Believer

In writing to the carnal, immature Corinthian believers, who were often divided in their fellowship by factions and schisms, and were prone to resort to human power struggles to get their own selfish way, Paul said,

> By the meekness and gentleness of Christ, I appeal to you—I, Paul,
> who am "timid" when face to face with You, but "bold" when
> away! (2 Cor. 10:1).

These Christians needed to grow in holiness, and in particular in the grace of humility. Humility is certainly high on God's list. He despises human pride, but blesses humility with His special grace (Prov. 3:34).

Only the regenerate may experience these grace virtues such as humility. It is a part of the cluster of the fruit of the Spirit, yet, as I have been saying, humility is an active concept. We must humble ourselves before God, *then* He responds in grace. Humility is our acknowledging who we are before God. If Jesus in humility acknowledged His dependence on the Father, how much more should we "frail creatures of dust"? As He was obedient unto death, how humbly should we obey God by our service to others?

The way to humility is, first, to come to Him in repentant, childlike faith to receive His forgiveness and saving grace. Then, we continue to come to Him in a growing personal relationship of taking upon ourselves His yoke of service (Matt. 11:29-30). We will grow in humility the more we understand Him and His nature. We become proud about ourselves and harsh with others when we compare ourselves with others. We might begin to think we're "somebody" because we might seem better than others in some way. But when we realize who we are in comparison with Jesus, we share the same sense of unworthiness Isaiah, Peter, and John sensed in His presence.

And we remain humble as we continue to depend on His grace and submit to His will. This we do by submitting to His Word, which is our authority (Jas. 1:21). We recognize the only way our lives are pleasing to Him is by our obedience to His specific commands given in His Word.

We grow in humility by our submission and service to one another in the Body of Christ (Jas. 3:17; 1 Pet. 5:5-7). We are to clothe ourselves with humility, as we seek to meet the needs of others and gently restore those who have fallen. Paul was perhaps concerned about the Galatians overreacting to his warning against the false teaching of the Judaizers. He listed humility and gentleness as part of the fruit of the Spirit, and gave the admonition of chapter 6 as if to say, "Be orthodox, but don't be mean; but be gentle and kind" (see Gal. 6:1-2).

Sometimes in our zeal for truth we forget that we can win an argument, and lose a friend; we can win the battle for truth, but trample upon precious lives. We must, like Jesus, put the needs of others first and serve them (Phil. 2:3*ff* and John 13:1*ff*). What a need there is today for humility and gentleness! These virtues would be the blessing of God on our church and in our homes.

Paul's marriage advice was based on the mutual humility and submission of husband and wife as fellow believers. In the context of this mutually submissive spirit the husband can assume his leadership role (Eph. 5:21*ff*). This humility would be the key to blessings in the home and church and also the answer to our effective witness in the world. Peter admonished wives to win their husbands to Christ through their humble submission (1 Pet. 3:1-7).

Also, our evangelism of the lost will not be done in the spirit of arrogance, of having all the answers. We are to

> be prepared to give an answer to everyone who asks you to give the reason for the hope that you have. But do this with gentleness and respect (1 Pet. 3:15).

As we humble ourselves before God and serve others in humble submission, we will be gentle and kind with those who are at our mercy. We will use our positions of authority (at work, home, or church) not to intimidate but to serve others. As we grow in this grace of the gentleness of Christ we will be approachable (2 Cor. 10:1). People will be at ease in our presence, even our children, employees, students, because they see we are humble before God and concerned about their well-being.

If you humble yourself as a husband and/or parent, God will exalt you to a position of an honored, respected, and loved spiritual leader. If you humble yourself to do the will of God revealed in His word, He will exalt your character to greater holiness, and you will inherit the fulness of His blessings here on earth and in the life to come. If you humble yourself as a servant in ministry, He will exalt your life, witness, and service unto His glory and your fruitfulness, rebounding to joy now and eternal rewards. If, on the other hand, you are arrogant, self-dependent, and resistant to God's will and work, you will find life turning to crush your spirit and dash your self-created ambitions and hopes.

Humility begins by submission to God's demand for repentance and seeking after His mercy and saving grace (Luke 18:9-14). But as we grow in grace we grow also in the grace of humility. Jesus said, "blessed are the meek (i.e., the humble and gentle), for they will inherit the earth" (Matt. 5:5). Those who are selfishly grabbing for life's real estate will someday be forced to relinquish it. But the obedient, submissive child of God possesses true riches now and looks forward to full access to the fulness of God's riches (1 Cor. 3:21-22).

Humility was expressed in the words of martyr-missionary Jim Elliott, who gave his life in humble service. He submitted himself even to those who brutally took his life, and wrote in his Bible, "He is no fool who gives up what he cannot keep to gain what he cannot lose!"[3]

Notes

1. W. E. Sangster, *The Pure in Heart,* (London: The Epworth Press, 1954) p. 158
2. Ibid
3. Elisabeth Elliott, *Through Gates of Splendor* (Wheaton, Ill.: Tyndale House Publishers, Inc., 1981), p. 172.

9

Holiness Is Self-Control

. . . the fruit of the Spirit is . . . self-control (Gal. 5:22-23).

Though I am free and belong to no man, I make myself a slave to everyone, to win as many as possible. To the Jews I became like a Jew, to win the Jews. To those under the law I became like one under the law (though I myself am not under the law), so as to win those under the law. To those not having the law I became like one not having the law (though I am not free from God's law but am under Christ's law), so as to win those not having the law. To the weak I became weak, to win the weak. I have become all things to all men so that by all possible means I might save some. I do all this for the sake of the gospel, that I may share in its blessings. Do you not know that in a race all the runners run, but only one gets the prize? Run in such a way as to get the prize. Everyone who competes in the games goes into strict training. They do it to get a crown that will not last; but we do it to get a crown that will last forever. Therefore I do not run like a man running aimlessly; I do not fight like a man beating the air. No, I beat my body and make it my slave so that after I have preached to others, I myself will not be disqualified for the prize (1 Cor. 9:19-27).

The final attribute that Paul listed in the cluster of the fruit of the Spirit is self-control (KJV, temperance). The call to holiness is the call to self-control. As with the other virtues, self-control is also demonstrated in the Deity.

The entire biblical record reveals the Lord God as holy and

perfect in His character, and under the control of His just and loving will. Even in His wrath and judgment against sin and sinners, He is not capricious or vindictive, but acts according to His predetermined and perfect will (2 Pet. 3:9). We see His self-control revealed in the Incarnate Christ, who was fully human as well as fully divine. Jesus was tempted in every way, including the temptation to lose control of His human appetites and temperament, "just as we are—yet was without sin" (Heb. 4:15).

Jesus felt strong temptations to indulge His natural appetites (e.g., in His wilderness temptations), yet sublimated these desires in order to do the will of God. Though He was often tempted to indulge His emotions in uncontrolled anger, yet His anger was always a righteous response to man's rejection of God's love, and was a controlled response calculated to reveal God's judgment (e.g., Mark 3:5). No doubt He also was tempted to indulge in self-pity or resentment when experiencing rejection, loneliness, and betrayal, yet Jesus' spirit remained under the control of His love and obedience to the will of His Heavenly Father. As with the other virtues, the Christian concept of self-control deserves special definition.

Definition of Self-Control

We have already noted that the world outside of Christ has its definitions of these concepts that for us describe the holy, separate life. Because holiness, simply stated, is the life of God implanted in the life of the believer, we cannot expect those who don't know God or know about His character to share the same definitions for these terms. Even as the world's definitions are different for words like "love," "joy," and "peace," so the world has its concept of self-control. Paul was writing to a people who recognized the value of practicing some kind of self-restraint, yet were attempting such on the basis of false assumptions.

Greek thought separated entirely the body from the soul, and believed that because the body was inherently wicked, it was to be either indulged (Epicurean) with no fear that it could contaminate a "perfect" soul, or it was to be denied (Stoics) and repressed as hopelessly evil. Such a life view is doomed to frustration, and certainly misses the goal that God has for us in creating us with appetites that are meant to be gratified in His way and in His time (1 Tim. 6:17).

The Christian's understanding of self-control is based on the assumption that the human body, with its appetites and inherent capabilities, was created by God. Even though sin has corrupted human nature, redemption through faith in Christ Jesus includes not only the immortal spirit, but also the body. These mortal bodies of flesh, which someday will be raised immortal and incorruptible, remain the battleground of Satan who wages war against us. Yet, we are indwelt by the Holy Spirit who gives us victory and exercises control over the sinful nature (Rom. 8:5-11).

The indwelling Holy Spirit enables us to exercise self-control. Perhaps we ought to speak of spirit-control rather than self-control. But self-control retains the sense of our responsibility to seek the dynamic of the Holy Spirit, who enables us to control the urges of mind and body.

The word self-control translates actually two Greek words which are important in our definition. One of these is the word for sound, spiritual wisdom, or mental self-control. Indeed, all self-control must begin with the mind, as we shall see. The other word emphasizes the inner strength of will, the actual and practical mastery of the self, in response to the mind, in the area of the body and the human spirit (or emotions). Self-control, then, is the ability with the aid of the Holy Spirit, to master the mental, physical, and emotional self to do what the spiritual mind directs us to do.

The Demand for Self-Control

The demand for self-control, as is true for the demand for entire holiness, is issued to us who are surrounded by unholiness and a society out of control. Jesus called us to follow Him in this world, to remain in it but to not be of it (John 17:15). Simon the Stylite was an eccentric believer in the early church who expressed his "discipleship" by sitting for thirty years or so on a pole, or a stile, to escape the contamination of the world.[1] That's one way, though not effective in terms of witness and service, to exercise self-control of appetites and passions. There are modern equivalents, such as the denomination whose Christian college claimed to have a good moral climate because it was ninety miles from the nearest known sin!

Self-control is demanded of us who must bear witness to those who know and care nothing about our ethical values. In a recent issue of a newsweekly, the cover story declared that the sexual revolution is over. Upon reading the article I gained the distinct impression that the sexual revolution of the past several decades has so altered acceptable moral standards that behavior once considered shocking and revolutionary is now status quo.

Tragically, as Paul discovered within the church at Corinth, there are believers who let the world into the church, that is, they begin to abandon self-control and let the world shape them into its mold of self-indulgence. The antinomian Gnostic influence that says "because the body is separate from the soul, immoral conduct in the body does not effect the soul" is still among some confessing Christians today. There are those who say that because their soul is saved, they don't have to worry about practicing self-control. The Word of God confronts them with the truth that whatever a Christian does is "unto the Lord," and affects his relationship with Christ, his testimony before others, and his influence on other Christians (Rom. 14).

The demand is not for a modern version of antinomianism or the other extreme—asceticism. God gave us our appetites, and as Paul told Timothy, has created everything and provided us "with everything for our enjoyment" (1 Tim. 6:17). In His own way and time, God intends to either gratify our appetites and desires, or to sublimate them, to give us the grace to subdue our appetites in order to serve Him in a particular way (e.g., the gift of celibacy allows single people to serve God in their singleness and remain sexually pure (1 Cor. 7). Usually, God allows us to satisfy our appetites in His way and time, whether for food to nourish our bodies, or the enjoyment of sex within marriage, which is His purpose. Paul said, regarding all appetites and desires, he as a believer would not allow himself to be mastered by anything. Rather, he would maintain self-control in order to serve God and edify others (1 Cor. 6:12).

The demand for self-control is the demand for a Spirit-controlled life. We realize the outside forces of temptation bombard us on every hand and pander to our every natural desire. We can see that "everybody else is doing it," that is, gratifying his or her every desire. We also can feel the downward pull of the sinful flesh. Yet, we know within us a greater power, that of the Holy Spirit, who is the Spirit of holiness. He will enable us to bring our appetites and our emotions under control as we follow the Lordship of Christ. Jesus' command to take up our cross (of self-denial) and follow Him is really a command to bring our conflicting desires under self-control, in order to be free to do His will. The demand is that we desire to live for the glory of God, that we desire His best for our lives rather than the fleeting pleasures of sin (1 Cor. 6:20).

Francis Schaeffer has noted that today's Western civilization is obsessed with the pursuit of immediate pleasure and gratification, but the Christian brings his life, including his desires, appetites and emotions, under control of the Holy Spirit that he might serve God and receive eternal reward.[2] For this "long look" Paul the apostle exercised strictest self-control, as an athlete in training, "to get a crown that will last forever" (1 Cor. 9:25).

The demand for self-control also includes the Christian's responsibility for his fellow-believer. We must be willing to control our desires and appetites, to relinquish what may in itself be permissible, in order to not offend a weaker brother (1 Cor. 8:31f).

Now that we understand the exacting demand for self-control, we are ready to engage in the discipline of self-control.

The Discipline of Self-Control

The championship-caliber athletes training for the Olympics are not lackadaisical about their training, but undergo the most rigorous self-discipline. Paul similarly brought his body under the severest self-control that he might not fail in his work and witness (1 Cor. 9:27).

Self-control necessarily begins in the mind, which is the control center for the body and emotions. Thus, the proverb urges us to guard the heart (the control center, i.e., the mind and will), "for it is the wellspring of life" (Prov. 4:23). We must with our minds exercise sound judgment and wisdom, which will dictate self-control (Prov. 29:11) over every area of our lives. Paul said that the ability to resist conformity to the baser standards of this world begins with the renewing of our minds (Rom. 12:2).

Along the same lines, the eye is the window of the mind, and the self-controlled believer must exercise discretion over what he views through that window. Obviously, we cannot avoid exposure to the enticements toward sin and self-indulgence in this age of unabashed corrupting of the flesh, yet we can and must keep our looking from becoming lusting. Martin Luther said that we can't keep the birds from flying over our heads, but we can keep them from building nests in our hair! Job wisely made a covenant with his eyes, "not to look lustfully at a girl" (Job 31:1). James showed us the importance of the mind as the potential "birthplace" of evil desire, which gives berth to overt sin (Ja. 1:14).

And, most sobering of all, our Lord Jesus taught us in His Sermon on the Mount that thoughts of injustified anger, contempt, and lust occasion the judgment of God as much as the overt fulfillment of those inner emotions and intentions (Matt. 5:21-30). Because self-control must begin with the mind, the believer must exercise discretion in his choice of literature, entertainment, companionship, and conversation. In an unguarded moment, Satan is able to conjure up an unclean thought out of the recesses of our memory of an impure joke or filthy word from an ill-advised conversation of long ago.

We ought to pray daily for the holy mind and attitude of our Lord and train ourselves to be godly thinkers which is the key to controlled conduct (2 Cor. 10:5; Phil. 2:5; 1 Tim. 4:7-8). Paul directed the Philippians, who needed to control their emotional tendency toward spiritual depression, to exercise self-controlled joy by thinking about things that are true, noble, right, pure, lovely, admirable, excellent, or praiseworthy (Phil. 4:8). Certainly, if we would limit our reflections to such lofty thoughts we would soon find ourselves out of depression and into rejoicing. I have found that nothing elevates my thoughts and gets me started each day in close fellowship with the Lord like time spent reading His Word and praising Him for His attributes. The psalmist asked,

> How can a young man keep the way pure? By living according to your word . . . I have hidden your word in my heart that I might not sin against you (Ps. 119:9,11).

With our minds determined to exercise self-control, we can follow the admonition to count ourselves "dead to sin but alive to God in Christ Jesus," and can offer to God our bodies as "instruments of righteousness" (Rom. 5:11-13). Now, by dependence upon the Holy Spirit, we can exercise self-control of the body, with its appetites and urges, and even with its lingering sinful nature (Rom. 8:9). Recognizing his need to exercise utmost self-control in order to be a consistent example to others and a faithful minister of Jesus Christ, Paul said, "I beat my body and make it my slave."

Because we serve God in and through our bodies, which are "instruments of righteousness," we must subject them to the best of care and stewardship. Rather than indulging our appetites, we are to exercise discipline in our eating, health habits, and physical exercise so that our bodies are honorable and healthy instruments of God. The obese, Bible-toting believer has forfeited his right to condemn the person addicted to tobacco. Bodily self-control not only includes the abstinence from the more notorious sins of sexual immorality and drunkenness, but also demands good time usage instead of laziness (e.g., excessive television watching, leisure spent in other nonproductive activity, and more than adequate sleep). Self-control includes controlling one's tongue against gossip, slander, or idle chatter (Jas. 3:1-12).

The use of fasting, though not unequivocally clear in Scripture, seems to have a place in the spiritual life of the Christian who engages in special seasons of prayer and search for a new spiritual understanding. Fasting can be an important disciplinary reminder that the Christian is to have mastery of his bodily appetites, and is to be mastered by none other than Christ Jesus, who is Lord of the body, and will chasten those who desecrate the temple of the Holy Spirit (1 Cor. 6:12-20).

Self-control also includes the discipline of the spirit, or the emotions. Those who are able to refrain from overt sins of the body are frequently vulnerable to the more subtle and socially (and religiously) acceptable sins of the spirit. The Bible clearly teaches that God views the sins of pride, contempt, hatred, and uncontrolled anger with seriousness equal to sins of the flesh: "Better a patient man than a warrior, a man who controls his temper than one who takes a city" (Prov. 16:32). One outburst of temper can negate years of positive influence, and bring loss of respect and alienation: "Like a city whose walls are broken down is a man who lacks self-control" (Prov. 25:28).

Not only must we control negative emotions toward others, such as resentment, bitterness, and contempt, but we must guard our feelings toward God and ourselves, which can cover the entire emotional gamut, including self-pity, unfounded guilt, and spiritual depression. Paul admonished the spiritually depressed and anxious to rejoice in the Lord and commanded them to pray trustfully rather than fret uselessly (Phil. 4:4-7). These believers whose emotions were out of control and out of God's will needed to exercise the discipline of love, rejoicing, and trust.

Conclusion

How difficult in our day yet how essential it is for the Christian to exercise self-control. We must first of all recognize that, no matter how we have failed in the past, we have but to confess and forsake those sins of intemperance. Also, regardless of how weak we may think of ourselves in light of our past failures and present weakness, we must realize we are not condemned to failure.

> Therefore, there is now no condemnation for those who are in Christ Jesus, because through Christ Jesus the law (principle) of the Spirit of life set me free from the law (principle, bondage) of sin and death.

Paul further said, "we do not live according to the sinful nature, but according to the Spirit" (Rom. 8:1-2,4b). We who are indwelt with the new nature created and empowered by the Holy Spirit have the means for self-control.

We need to ask God to show us our sins and weaknesses that are out of His control (Ps. 139:23). Once seeing these areas of danger, we must wisely take refuge in His grace and strength (Prov. 27:12). We must not dally with temptation in these areas, but flee from dangerous desires (2 Tim. 2:22) and give the devil no opportunity to defeat us. We need to learn to live in the balance of fear and faith, caution and confidence as we . . . "continue to work out (our) salvation with fear and trembling" (Phil. 2:12).

We tremble as we consider our weakness, and the power of temptation, and the power of the enemy. We fear the prospects that Paul feared, that by the loss of self-control we might become disqualified as God's useful and rewarded servants (1 Cor. 9:27) We cannot be too cautious, thus we work out our salvation with fear and trembling. Yet, we must also balance this caution with the confidence that Paul expressed in the following verse of the Philippian passage: "For it is God who works in you to will and to act according to his purpose" (Phil. 2:13).

Notes

1. W. E. Sangster, *The Pure in Heart,* (London: The Epworth Press, 1954), pp. 176-177

2. Francis A. Schaeffer, *The Great Evangelical Disaster,* (Westchester, N.Y.: Crossway Books, 1984), pp. 62-63.

10

Growing in Holiness, Step One: "Go to the Helper"

One of the most popular books among Christians of the past two decades has been *The Key to Triumphant Living: An Adventure in Personal Discovery.* In it, author Jack Taylor shared his pilgrimage from the realm of struggle into new discoveries of faith. He wrote, "My father was a farmer and a very good one. I suppose that I simply deduced that if my father could become a good farmer by hard work, I could become a good Christian in the same manner."[1] Taylor's testimonial book relates his discovery that spiritual victory is not achieved by human effort but rather has already been achieved for us by Christ, through His death and resurrection. The key to triumphant living is found in our relationship of dependence upon Christ within us, who is our hope of glory (Col. 1:27).

God has called us not just to personal spiritual victory, but to a life of holiness. We are called not only to experience personal joy, but also to bring glory to God. I will never experience personal fulfilment nor will I fulfil the purposes of God for my life until I answer this call to holiness. Our study of holiness, as portrayed by the fruit of the Spirit, presents us with a desirable but demanding set of standards. I can thank God for any spiritual growth in my life. Because His Spirit has been faithfully at work within me since my childhood conversion, there has been some degree of progress even during those long seasons of my life when I was not actively seeking spiritual development. I now rejoice that God has stirred up within me a greater desire to grow into such degrees of holiness that will allow me to more clearly and fully see the Lord (Heb. 12:14). I know that as I, by faith, can more fully and clearly perceive His nature I will desire to share more of His nature (2 Cor. 3:18). A great example for us in this desire to grow in holiness is the apostle Paul, whose lifetime ambition was to more fully know Christ and the power of His resurrection and conformity to His character (Phil. 3:10*ff*).

The study of Christlikeness, of the character of holiness as outlined in the fruit of the Spirit passage, impresses us that holiness must be a dynamically progressive experience. We cannot honestly examine God's standards for our holiness and be satisfied with our spiritual attainments. On the other hand, perhaps we feel somewhat overwhelmed and a little dizzy by the height of the upward call of Christlikeness.

I think of the story about the recent graduate of agricultural college who began offering unsolicited advice to an experienced farmer. The old farmer interrupted the upstart's lecture with, "Young man, I already know more about farming than I'm doing!" Perhaps we sense by now that we know more about holiness than we are experiencing. What are the steps to experiencing what we know and desire? The old farmer knew he could do a better job of farming by working harder at what he already knew to do. But, as Jack Taylor discovered, spiritual growth and success are not produced by the same formula as agricultural success. Certainly, we must "roll up the sleeves" of our spiritual minds, and diligently obey the truths of God's Word, but human effort alone will result in failure and frustration. Many Christians know much more than they are willing, or feel able, to do.

Perhaps the place to begin is to acknowledge either our spiritual neglect or disobedience which have resulted in our failure to grow as God intends us to grow in holiness. With this admission we are ready to take the first step, which is going to the Helper.

My dear children, I write this to you so that you will not sin. But
if anybody does sin, we have One who speaks to the Father in our
defense—Jesus Christ, the Righteous One. He is the atoning sacrifice for our sins, and not only for ours but also for the sins of the
whole world (1 John 2:1-2).

The apostle John, in the first chapter of his First Epistle, spoke
to the inherent sinfulness of all persons, and God's provision for
the cleaning of sins (1 John 1:5-10). It seems that John anticipated
two false conclusions drawn from what he had just said, and in
1 John 2:1-2, he dealt with them. The first false assumption might
be, "Since Jesus' blood cleanses us from all sins, we might as well
sin as much as we wish." The apostle Paul also had to confront this
antinomian heresy (Rom. 6:1-2). The other false conclusion seems
to be, "Since we are destined to repeatedly sin in this life, there
is no hope to become holy and Christlike, therefore we give up the
struggle." John noted that, yes, believers will sin, and if they are
true believers, they will sin *more* than they want to. True Christians
hate *all* and *any* sin, and realizing God's provision for forgiveness
and holiness, will not grow discouraged but will be encouraged to
confess and forsake sin and grow in Christlikeness.

How important is the attitude and approach of the apostle John
as he confronted those under his care with their sins and spiritual
failure. In this Pastoral Epistle we note the Spirit-inspired balance
of confrontation and kindness. We in the church today, particularly in places of leadership, need to be on guard against severity on
one hand and leniency on the other. We tend to be either too harsh
and judgemental or too soft and sentimental regarding sin in our
own lives and in those of our fellow Christians. Generally, the
need is to be harsher with ourselves and more lenient toward
others, since we cannot know all their circumstances.

With Spirit-inspired balance John addressed his confrontational
epistle to the believers in Asia Minor, whom he lovingly regarded
as his "little children." *Teknia* was an appropriate appellation for

those whom John may have himself led to Christ. It is also likely that John, at the time of his writing being "a veritable patriarch in age," was considerably older and wiser than most of his readership.[2]

His intense love for them earned him the right to admonish them to fulfil their calling to become holy as Jesus is holy. He wrote that they sin not, that they continue to grow in holiness until they reach perfection. Not that they shall be sinlessly perfect in this life, but that they progress toward that mark of being perfect as is our Heavenly Father (Matt. 5:48). He wrote that they sin not. He admonished sinlessness, but realistically noted that we who remain in the flesh will commit particular sins from time to time. The Greek tense is the aorist, for completed, punctiliar action.[3] "If anyone does sin," or rather, "when you do sin, this is what you must do, and these things you must know."

Jesus taught us to daily confess sin and ask for forgiveness (Matt. 6:12) for sins we have committed—sins of the flesh, mind, and spirit—things we have done and things we have failed to do which we should have done. When we sin, we cannot be happy with our sin, and we will not go on habitually continuously sinning as we did prior to our conversion (as we noted in 1 John 3:4) because this pattern of sin is not of our new nature. Chastening because He loves us

> Our fathers disciplined us for a little while as they thought best; but God disciplines us for our good, that we may share in His holiness. No discipline seems pleasant at the time, but painful. Later on, however, it produces a harvest of righteousness and peace for those who have been trained by it (Heb. 12:10-11).

We are now the sheep of His pasture, and a sheep may fall into the mud but he will not remain in the mud to wallow in it like a hog will do. It is the nature of a hog to wallow in the mud, as it is the nature of an unconverted sinner to remain in his sins.

With pastoral kindness John encouraged his flock to not be

dishearted and discouraged because they have committed occasional sins and have obviously failed to live up to their call to holiness. The Holy Spirit will make us uncomfortable with our sin, but as John instructed, there are definite steps we can take.

Go to the Helper

When you sin, John said, remember that you have an Advocate. This Greek word *paraclētos* means, "one called to the side of another to help," and in this context has a forensic meaning. When a person is in legal trouble he often will go to a legal advocate, a lawyer, and seek his services in presenting his case to the court.

When we sin, we are to remember we have an Advocate, Jesus Christ the Righteous One, who takes our case before the court of heaven. Jesus Christ, the Eternal Son of God, the perfectly sinless (*dikaios*) One, is qualified to handle our case of sin against the Heavenly Father—His Moral Law, and His requirements of holiness and obedience. He alone has underived access to the throne of the Heavenly Father, to whom He presents our case.

The moment we sinned there was a prosecuting attorney who promptly and gleefully went to the Father to accuse us and to condemn our conscience. His name is Satan (Rev. 12:10). He told the Father all about our sins and that we should be condemned to hell because of them. This prosecutor—Satan—lies to us and tells us we "really blew·it" when we sinned by losing our temper or giving way to a particular temptation.

But, no sooner did he accuse us than Jesus, our risen, glorified High Priest, stood before the Father and made intercession for us as our Advocate (Heb. 7:25). He said something like, "Father, that sin about which Satan told You—I died for that sin, shed My blood for that sin as You appointed Me to do before the foundation of the world. Father, that person, Bill (or Jane), he is one of Your children of grace whom You chose from before the foundation of the world. My blood has cleansed all his sin and the sin debt is paid. He is in me, and I am in you" (John 17:21).

As Calvin said, Jesus turns the Father's gaze away from the sin toward His own righteousness. And the loving Father smiles upon us because He sees us as righteous as His own Beloved Son.[4]

A great illustration of this ongoing scenario of grace was described by the prophet Zechariah (3:1-7). The prophet had a vision soon after the Israelites' return from Exile of the high priest Joshua, who symbolized the nation Israel, which had sinned against the Lord. Joshua is before the heavenly court and is clad in filthy garments, indicative of his and the people's sins. Satan, the prosecuting attorney, stands to accuse Joshua, but Joshua had an Advocate who stood at God's right hand. This Advocate, whom we know to be Christ, gave to Joshua a change of garments and thereby silenced the accusations of Satan. We also have received the white robes of our righteousness (Rev. 7:13).

John said, "we have an Advocate with the Father, Jesus Christ the Righteous." Jesus goes to the Father on our behalf before we are even stirred by conscience to confess our sins. We have an Advocate regardless of what we do. We are not only justified by His grace but also our continuing, our perseverance, is of grace. When we sin as Christians there still is nothing in *our* goodness or by our efforts that can warrant forgiveness. We can but receive His gracious gift of righteousness, of right standing with the Father.

But to enjoy fellowship with the Father we must confess, that is, agree with the Holy Spirit that what we have done or failed to do is sin. We come boldly to the throne of grace to receive mercy and find grace to help (Heb. 4:16). We confess our sins, and He faithfully and justly forgives and cleanses us (1 John 1:9). We can now go to the Helper to receive His gift.

Receive His Gift

There is nothing we can do but humbly receive what He has provided for us. To have fellowship with the Father we must acknowledge and gratefully receive what He has given.

A child's disobedience does not totally destroy his or her relationship with the parent, but the child can damage the fellowship with that parent until the child agrees what he or she has done is wrong and asks forgiveness. In the same way, at issue is not the possibility of losing our relationship as the children of God. Instead, we seek the gift of forgiveness in order to maintain and strengthen our fellowship with the Father.

John went deeper behind the thought of verse one when in the second verse he reminded us of the supreme work of Christ, His sacrificial death that made possible our forgiveness, and His continuing work of intercession on our behalf. We can go to the Helper to receive His gift of forgiveness because of what He has done for us.

Many communities have a Legal Aid Society, a socially-funded legal service for the economically disadvantaged. We also were too poor to pay, too much in debt to the Father, so He provided Jesus Christ to be the "propitiation for our sins."

John, like the writer of the book of Hebrews, presented Jesus as our Great High Priest. Here, Jesus is not only the High Priest but He is also the sacrifice, the propitiation (*hilasmos*) for our sins.

This concept is taken from the Old Testament sacrifice for sins annually performed by the high priest on the Day of Atonement. He sacrificed the animal and poured the blood of the sacrifice on the Mercy Seat (*hilasterion,* Heb. 9:5; Rom. 3:25), the place where holy God met to forgive the sins of the repentant Israelites. With that sacrifice made with repentant hearts God's wrath against sin was abated, or propitiated, and His justice was satisfied.

Much of the modern scholarship rejects the concept of propitiation, preferring instead the concept of expiation, i.e., the covering of sin (as in the Revised Standard Version translation and C. H. Dodd's "removal of the taint of sin").[5] Such theological aversion abhors the connotation of God's anger with the sinner and need for His wrath to be abated. Granted, the biblical witness rejected the association that "expiation-proponents" fear, i.e., the association of the holy God with the pagan dieties, who were capricious and uncontrolled in their anger, and in constant need of being placated from their vindictive, whimsical actions. The God of the Bible, on the other hand, is a God of just, righteous, and controlled wrath against sin. Not only does the sinner need to be reconciled to God, but God to the sinner, who has willfully violated the holy and loving nature and commandments of God (Rom. 5:1-11).

But God, unlike the pagan dieties, takes the initiative of reconciliation and out of His perfect love provides the propitiation, that is, for the satisfaction of his justice and wrath against sin (1 John 4:10). God is holy and cannot overlook sin, yet because He gave His only Son to be that sacrifice He is both just and the Justifier of those who believe in Jesus (Rom. 3:26). God, because of His love, met His own demands for righteousness, and gave Jesus as the eternal sacrifice through His death, which never has to be nor can be repeated. Because He is love, God yearns to forgive all. His sacrifice, John said, is "for the sins of the whole world" (verse 2).

The gracious provisions of Jesus' death, which we celebrate in the ordinance of the Lord's Supper, was a sacrifice, a sin payment, for all the sins of the world. "He so loved the *world* that He gave His Son" (John 3:16). But the benefits of this sacrifice are received only by repentance and faith. Paul said that God put forth Jesus as a propitiation (*hilasterion*) by His blood "to be received by faith" (Rom. 3:25). Only the children of God have received this amazing gift, and the benefits of this gift remain forever. Our sins are covered by His blood, completely paid for. We freely go to the Helper, our Advocate, who continues to represent our case to the Father on the merits of *His gift.*

Thus did John, the pastor-apostle, gently but powerfully confront the false conclusions to his presentation of the gospel truth. Forgiveness is indeed free to us, but it is not *cheap* grace.[6] God forbid that we who have died to sin (sin's penalty and dominant power) continue to live in it. It's against our new nature, our new "want to." We have a new gratitude to God and appreciation for His grace through Jesus' great sacrifice. By His shed blood we have received forgiveness, and by His suffering and death the gift of Eternal Life. We have a new calling, to be as righteous as Jesus is righteous, and to a new grace and power through our Advocate. Jesus said that the Holy Spirit, who indwells every believer, is our abiding Advocate. The presence of the indwelling Christ is to teach us the Word, to have fellowship with us, lead and empower us for Christlikeness (the fruit of the Spirit), and to give us a fruitful, evangelistic witness. Thus, because every believer is given the Holy Spirit, no one can rightfully be overwhelmed, defeated, or even discouraged about living a godly, victorious life.

The call to each one of us is a call issued to beloved children, saved by grace and precious in His sight, to learn to agree with God about the occasional sins we commit, and to confess and forsake them, knowing that our Advocate, Jesus, has already been to the Father in our behalf. In the first step toward holiness, we need to begin on a clean slate.

I ask you, my reader, to join me at the feet of our Advocate, Jesus Christ. Let's agree with Him about our sins, which have stunted our growth in holiness. Let's turn a deaf ear to our accuser, Satan, who would dishearten us. We know we have a higher calling. For this purpose Christ died for us and called us to grace that we might be "holy and blameless in his sight" (Eph. 1:4).

> If we confess our sins, He is faithful and just and will forgive us our sins and purify us from all unrighteousness (1 John 1:9).

Once we know the joy and peace of forgiveness and restored fellowship with the Father, we are ready for step two.

Notes

1. Jack R. Taylor, *The Key to Triumphant Living: An Adventure in Personal Discovery* (Nashville: Broadman Press, 1971), p. 19.

2. John R. W. Stott, *The Epistles of John: An Introduction and Commentary* (Grand Rapids, Mich.: Wm. B. Eerdmans Publishing Co., 1975), p. 40.

3. Archibald Thomas Robertson, *Word Pictures in the New Testament,* v. VI (Nashville: Sunday School Board of the S.B.C., 1933), p. 209.

4. John Calvin, *Calvin's New Testament Commentaries,* v. 5, translated by T. H. L. Parker (Grand Rapids, Mich.: Wm. B. Eerdmans Publishing Co., 1959), p. 243.

5. I. Howard Marshall, *The Epistles of John* (Grand Rapids, Mich.: Wm. B. Eerdmans Publishing Co., 1978), pp. 118-119.

6. Dietrich Bonhoeffer, *The Cost of Discipleship,* revised edition (New York: The Macmillan Co., 1963), pp. 45-60.

11

Growing in Holiness, Step Two: "Live by the Spirit"

Now that we have gone to the Helper, and received the gift of His forgiveness and fellowship, we look forward with joy to the next step that brings us even closer to our goal of conformity to the character of our Lord Jesus Christ. The challenge in taking step one may have been that of overcoming our pride. We acknowledged the call to holiness was beyond the realm of human possibility, and had to admit our failure to achieve holiness. We then sought the restoration of our fellowship with God. That was perhaps the negative step, the one that allowed God to graciously negate our sin that blocked our fellowship with Him. Throughout our earthly pilgrimage, til we reach our final destiny beyond this mortal life, we will need to continually exercise this initial step.

The four steps toward holiness are like a military march in 4/4 time, with four beats to each measure. Our growth toward holiness is measured by disciplined steps, beginning with our seeking God's gracious forgiveness. Because of our inherent weakness we must repeatedly take the first step of restoring and maintaining our fellowship with God. Step two takes us beyond the place of forgiveness and into the fulness of life by the Holy Spirit.

The fruit of the Spirit passage, which was our focus for understanding the nature of holiness, is set in the context of Paul's admonition to the Galatians to live their lives according to the influence of the Holy Spirit. The Galatian letter is a treatise on true

110

Christian liberty, the life of freedom to be a loving, serving child of God, free from the bondage of institutional legalism and also the downward tug of the sinful nature. The key to this freedom, and the way of attaining the life of holiness described as the fruit of the Spirit, is to live by the Spirit.

> You, my brothers, were called to be free. But do not use your freedom to indulge the sinful nature; rather, serve one another in love. The entire law is summed up in a single command: "Love your neighbor as yourself." If you keep on biting and devouring each other, watch out or you will be destroyed by each other. So I say, live by the Spirit, and you will not gratify the desires of the sinful nature. For the sinful nature desires what is contrary to the Spirit, and the Spirit what is contrary to the sinful nature. They are in conflict with each other, so that you do not do what you want. But if you are led by the Spirit, you are not under law. The acts of the sinful nature are obvious: sexual immorality, impurity and debauchery; idolatry and witchcraft; hatred, discord, jealousy, fits of rage, selfish ambition, dissensions, factions and envy; drunkenness, orgies, and the like. I warn you, as I did before, that those who live like this will not inherit the kingdom of God. But the fruit of the Spirit is love, joy, peace, patience, kindness, goodness, faithfulness, gentleness and self-control. Against such things there is no law. Those who belong to Christ Jesus have crucified the sinful nature with its passions and desires. Since we live by the Spirit, let us keep in step with the Spirit (Gal. 5:13-25).

The key expression of this passage is "live by the Spirit," which is the modern English equivalent of the literal translation of the original expression, "walk in the Spirit" (as translated in the King James Version). Perhaps our more modern translations, for sake of modern equivalency, have sacrificed something of the poignancy of this original word picture. "Walking" is a biblical metaphor for one's conduct and pattern of behavior, and the concept of walking with someone expresses compatible conduct and a cordial relationship with another.

The prophet Amos expressed this principle with the question, "Do two walk together unless they have agreed to do so?" (Amos 3:3). Though little is said about the ancient Enoch we can conclude much about his character of godliness because of the statement that he "walked with God" (Gen. 5:24). Since the Holy Spirit is the third person of the Triune God we can conclude that Paul was exhorting a similar walk with God, living in a compatible, close relationship with the One who indwells us in the person of the Holy Spirit.

In commenting on this text (Gal. 5:13-25) New Testament scholar F. F. Bruce suggested a nuance in meaning between living and walking by the Spirit. "Walking by the Spirit is the outward manifestation, in action and speech, of living by the Spirit. Living by the Spirit is the root. Walking by the Spirit is the fruit." He said that the fruit is the practical reproduction of the character and conduct of Christ in the lives of His people![1] As we live according to the direction and control of the Holy Spirit, in agreement with God's Word and will we shall then walk in step with the Spirit, who will produce in our lives the fruit of the Spirit (vv. 22-23), which we recognize as the essence of holiness.

The second step toward holiness is one that puts us in stride with the Holy Spirit, who is the Agent and Enabler in our march toward attaining God's purpose for our lives.

Barriers to Holiness

By way of contrast Paul listed certain acts of the sinful nature. This sordid list (vv. 19-21) describes the results of giving free rein to the old, preconversion sin nature. As we have already noted, the born-again child of God will not continue those same patterns of sinful conduct. But we know that, as long as we live in this sin-inclined bodies, we will feel the downward tug of the old nature. In moments of weakness, when we are not living in the fulness of God's protective grace and presence (living in step with the Spirit), we will commit particular sins. Maybe not as sordid as these in

Paul's list, and perhaps they will be sins of attitude or sins of inaction, i.e., failure to act in response to the promptings of God's Word and Spirit. But we know what to do. We go to the Helper, our Advocate, who cleanses us and frees us once again to go on to the productive and joyful life of living and walking by the Spirit.

Perhaps one of the most difficult facts for a new convert to accept is that, although we are given a new nature and become God's new creation at conversion, we still must engage in continual warfare against the remaining tendencies from our old nature. The flesh as Paul used the term, is the part of us that continues to wage conflict against our new nature and our life in the Spirit.

This does not mean that the body, as separate from the Spirit, is inherently evil, as some of the Gnostic Greeks believed. The flesh is that part of us that still feels the downward tug of our preconversion life. Though our entire being has come under God's grace and redemptive power and is being gradually transformed by the Spirit into His likeness, we still must resist the inclinations of old patterns, habits, attitudes, and emotions that are against God's new purposes. The old nature, as an echo of the past, still haunts us as the voice of Satan, the accuser, trying to interrupt our spiritual growth.

The atmosphere of the world around us, such as the conduct and conversations of immoral and insensitive folk with whom we must live or work, can incite these old desires and tempt us to a momentary return to these acts of the sinful nature ("works of the flesh," KJV). Jerry Bridges has aptly described these recurring struggles as the Christians continuing "Guerrilla Warfare."[2] The battle for the soul has been won decisively. We now belong to Christ and have the victory described by Paul in Romans 8.

But enough of the enemy remain around to engage us in the occasional skirmishes that continue to disturb and threaten to defeat us, as expressed in Romans 7. The process of breaking the patterns of occasional defeat begins with going to the Helper for

His gracious forgiveness. Then with new resolve we must abstain from the sinful desires that war against our souls (1 Pet. 2:11). With the barriers to the life in the Spirit now surmounted by God's grace and superior power, we are ready to begin or perhaps resume, a joyful walk in the Spirit.

Holiness is a joint venture between God and His children. By grace God provides all we need for life and godliness (2 Pet. 1:3). But we must will and work for our holiness with the full concentration of our spiritual energies. Charles Colson put it quite simply when he said that holiness is the toughest vocation in the world.[3] Holiness involves, as we noted from 1 Peter 1:13, preparing our minds for action. Paul says we must set our minds on things above and not on the earthly (Col. 3:2). We must put our mental powers to work, applying Scriptural truth and principles to our lives. Then, with the full engagement of our will and determination we must rid ourselves of the old patterns:

> Put to death, therefore, whatever belongs to your earthly nature: sexual immorality, impurity, lust, evil desires and greed, which is idolatry. Because of these, the wrath of God is coming. You used to walk in these ways, in the life you once lived. But now you must rid yourselves of all such things as these: anger, rage, malice, slander, and filthy language from your lips. Do not lie to each other, since you have taken off your old self with its practices and have put on the new self, which is being renewed in knowledge in the image of its Creator. Here there is no Greek or Jew, circumcised or uncircumcised, barbarian, Scythian, slave or free, but Christ is all, and is in all (Col. 3:5-11).

The Goal of Holiness

With these barriers to holiness behind us, we must move toward the positive goal of our holiness. Adding to the image of walking in the Spirit is the concept of clothing ourselves with holiness.

Therefore, as God's chosen people, holy and dearly loved, clothe yourselves with compassion, kindness, humility, gentleness and patience. Bear with each other and forgive whatever grievances you may have against one another. Forgive as the Lord forgave you. And over all these virtues put on love, which binds them all together in perfect unity (Col. 3:12-14).

We know unequivocally that God has called us to a life of holiness. No longer can we plead ignorance to the primacy and urgency of this calling. We know also it is a tough vocation, a calling to a life that demands discipline and determination to be holy.

Perhaps now is the time to put this book aside and get alone with God, asking yourself, "Am I willing to answer this call to be holy? To accept the goals to live the only kind of life that honors God? To enter into the kind of spiritual discipline that will allow me to see God, to understand Him, and fellowship with Him as never before?"

Now, with the assurance there is really no option to obedience and no substitute for God's fullest blessings, we are ready to move toward the goal of holiness that is reached by living in the Spirit. The goal of holiness is no less than reaching the measure of total Christlikeness. This is what God's grace reaches in us. Certainly, we by grace are saved from hell and bound for heaven, but we are saved for the larger purpose of glorifying God by reflecting His nature (Rom. 8:29).

By walking in the Spirit, living in concert with God's will and Word, we become more like Jesus day by day (2 Cor. 3:18). It's the gradual process that involves our cooperation with God and results in our conformity to God. It's the way we begin obeying the command of our Lord to be perfect as our Father in heaven is perfect (Matt. 5:48). The fulfillment of that requirement will be reached only when we see Jesus face to face, but we begin the process immediately (1 John 3:2). The goal of our holiness starts and ends with God's grace, but includes our willingness to let the

Holy Spirit sanctify us (make us holy) "through and through" (1 Thess. 5:23). God's goal for us is the sancitification of our entire lives, all that we are and all that we have.

In the Old Testament, not only were people made holy, but so were tabernacles, temples, and articles used in worship and service. The goal of our entire sanctification, that comes by our living according to the Spirit, must include all we are and also all we have. We need to submit to God's control and the Lordship of Christ all of our possessions and relationships. We may recognize there are many things beyond our control, such as our job environment, or even family and other interpersonal relationships that include persons unsympathetic with our Christian calling. Yet, as we seek the full control of the Holy Spirit and the Lordship of Christ in our lives we will discover the evidence of God's influence upon our circumstances and relationships. Perhaps it is to this principle Paul was speaking when he says that "the unbelieving husband has been sanctified through his (believing) wife" (1 Cor. 7:14).

The goal of holiness is that all our life, relationships, possessions and influence be permeated with the presence of God. When God can be made known through our lives then we are beginning to reach the goal of holiness, which is the glory of God. The title of the B. B. McKinney hymn says it all, "Let Others See Jesus in You."[4] Jesus said, "Let your light shine before men that they may see your good deeds and praise your Father in heaven" (Matt. 5:16).

In commenting on 2 Cor. 3:18, "And we, who with unveiled faces all reflect the Lord's glory, are being transformed into His likeness with ever-increasing glory, which comes from the Lord, who is the Spirit," J. Sidlow Baxter said that even as Moses' face reflected the glory of God so should the countenance of the Christian indicate the presence of the Spirit of his or her life.[5] Not that there is a halo or glow visible to every undiscerning eye, but the expression on the face of the one who walks in full fellowship with God ought to radiate something of the authentic presence of God's peace and joy.

This is not something to be forced or that can even be produced by conscious effort. Few things are more irritating and inauthentic than the gushy exhuberance of a superficial Christian "superstar." Those who reflect God in their countenance may not have much natural beauty but unconsciously reflect the beauty of a life filled with God. "Blessed are the pure in heart, for they will see God," and it is not unlikely that we can see the evidence of this contemplation in their faces (Matt. 5:8). These are the kind of people I long to be like. This is, I have discovered, my highest goal.

The Way of Holiness

The way of holiness, simply put, is the walk in the Spirit, to live in dependence upon His presence and influence. It is the life of deliberate and disciplined identification with the Savior, as Paul said, being crucified with Christ (Gal. 2:20). It is realizing that the power of the old nature which used to dominate us is now subdued under the power of God invested in our new nature. We now may rightfully claim for our own lives the very power of God that raised Christ Jesus from the dead (Eph. 1:19-20).

The way of holiness, living and walking in the Spirit, becomes our way of life as we begin to practice spiritual disciplines outlined in the Word of God. In his practical letters to a young minister, Timothy, Paul admonished the disciplined exercise of godliness, which far surpassed the value of physical training in that it holds "promise for both the present life and the life to come" (1 Tim. 4:8). The way of holiness involves the effort of our participation in God-provided means for spiritual discipline and growth.

Richard Foster, though writing from a Quaker perspective, gave a helpful and clear delineation of the disciplines God has provided and commanded for our spiritual growth and useful service.[6] The emphasis of the Keswic movement and conferences has been, at least in the opinion of one astute theologian, a more passive approach to holiness that centers on our personal spiritual victory by simply "letting go and letting God."[7] A more biblical view, it seems to me, must balance God's provision of grace and enabling power with our responsibility to practice the disciplines of personal spiritual growth and active Christian service. The focus of the more balanced approach is on the glory of God rather than the secret of spiritual success or felicity.

The way of holiness is the way of a balanced dependence upon God and the resources of His grace, along with a determination to, in the phrase of the Puritans, attend to the means of grace, to practice the disciplines necessary for our growth in holiness. Through the regular and meaningful practice of personal worship (i.e., prayer, Bible study, and meditation), corporate worship, and Christian service in and to a lost and needy world, I will be maintaining my walk in the Spirit and will keep in step with the Spirit in the march toward holiness. We must be on guard against the loss of this balance. We must continue to work out our salvation with fear and trembling (Phil. 2:12). That's our part. But we must not forget it is God who works in us to will and to act according to His good purpose (Phil. 4:13).

The call to holiness is so demanding and challenging we approach it with fear and trembling. Yet the goal that beckons and the God who calls us leave us no choice but to follow the call to the very end. But as we march toward our glorious goal, let us not forget our brothers and sisters in Christ. They too have been called to holiness.

Notes

1. F. F. Bruce, *The Epistle to the Galatians* (Grand Rapids, Mich.: Wm. B. Eerdmans Publishing Co., 1982), p. 257.
2. Jerry Bridges, *The Pursuit of Holiness* (Colorado Springs, Colo.: NavPress, 1978), p. 70.

3. Charles W. Colson, *Loving God* (Grand Rapids, Mich.: Zondervan Publishing House, 1983), p. 122.

4. © Copyright 1924. Renewal 1952 Broadman Press. All rights reserved.

5. J. Sidlow Baxter, *Christian Holiness Restudied and Restated* (Grand Rapids, Mich.: Zondervan Publishing House, 1977), pp. 166-169.

6. Richard Foster, *Celebration of Discipline: The Path to Spiritual Growth* (New York: Harper & Row, Publishers, 1978)

7. James I. Packer, *Keep in Step with the Spirit* (Old Tappan, N.J.: Fleming H. Revell Company, 1984), p. 151.

12
Growing in Holiness, Step Three: "Continue to the End"

Our march toward holiness is in 4/4 time, and if we should skip a beat we will get out of cadence and find ourselves waltzing in 3/4 time. I think of a march as a bright, determined progression toward a definite destination. By contrast, a waltz seems to me more of an entertaining but meandering sort of motion, a pleasant exercise, but without a particular destination in mind. Without a proper consideration of our responsibilities beyond our personal holiness we run the risk of justifying much of the criticism leveled against holiness teaching and preaching.

Some, even in the evangelical ranks, have little use for an emphasis on holiness teaching because of their perception that all who strongly propound attention to personal holiness do so at the expense of evangelistic activity or social involvement. No doubt some in the Puritan-Pietist tradition have deserved this criticism, but not those who adhere to the balance of biblical teaching.[1] The call to holiness is the call to concern for all that glorifies God, including the righteousness of all of society as well as our personal holiness.

The church is the community of the people of God called to do the work of God's active righteousness in the world. The only way to keep our pursuit of holiness from lapsing into a lackadaisical waltz of self-centered pietism is to remember the church and realize our part in it.

Therefore, rid yourselves of all malice and all deceit, hypocrisy, envy, and slander of every kind. Like newborn babies, crave pure spiritual milk, so that by it you may grow up in your salvation, now that you have tasted that the Lord is good. As you come to him, the living Stone—rejected by men but chosen by God and precious to him—you also, like living stones, are being built into a spiritual house to be a holy priesthood, offering spiritual sacrifices acceptable to God through Jesus Christ. For in Scripture it says:

> "See, I lay a stone in Zion,
>   a chosen and precious cornerstone,
>   and the one who trusts in him
>   will never be put to shame."

Now to you who believe, this stone is precious. But to those who do not believe,

> "The stone the builders rejected
>   has become the capstone,"

and

> "A stone that causes men to stumble
>   and a rock that makes them fall."

They stumble because they disobey the message—which is also what they were destined for. But you are a chosen people, a royal priesthood, a holy nation, a people belonging to God, that you may declare the praises of him who called you out of darkness into his wonderful light. Once you were not a people, but now you are the people of God; once you had not received mercy, but now you have received mercy (1 Pet. 2:1-10).

I will never forget my visit to my good friend's little church during my last semester of college, as I was beginning to get some preaching experience before entering seminary. This was a high attendance day and the atmosphere was charged with excitement. Helium-filled balloons covered the ceiling of the sanctuary as children from nine months to ninety years of age gathered, each one hoping they had broken their Sunday School attendance record. If so, Pastor Tim would break another record, a phonograph record over the Sunday School superintendent's very bald head.

The attendance record was broken, so the gangly gentleman submissively bent over so my short preacher-friend could summarily break his record over that bare skull. Imagine the hilarity in the place as Tom beat and bent over that poor man's head what proved to be an unbreakable record! I must have thought, "Am I going to seminary to study theology and prepare for a ministry that will require a course in circus performance?"

Don't misunderstand. We ought to use methods and motivations, with integrity, that are consistent with our purpose and will encourage people to belong and to work through the church. Also, any who know me realize that I, like my friend, Tom, love to have fun in church. And, by the way, Tom is today a dynamic pastor with a biblical, integral ministry. What concerns me is that, if your church attendance, membership, and service are powered soley by exciting events and catchy slogans, sooner or later the program will run out of gas. That record-breaking contest was a hard act to follow. Only a pastor as creative as my friend could pull it off! Also, those helium-filled balloons would go over today in some parts of the country and the world like one giant lead balloon. Where it really costs something to be a professing Christian and a church member one must appeal to higher and stronger motives. I believe the day is coming, particularly in the Western world, when church entertainment, no matter how classy, will no longer "bring them in."

The apostle Peter wrote to the churches of Asia Minor, under the ominous shadow of Roman persecution, to remind them why they had made that costly choice to follow Jesus Christ and to be publicly identified with His people, the church.

Called to Be His People

Peter reminded his readers that there was a time when they, because of their alienation from God, had lost their identity. Spiritually, they were "nobodies," but now they are "a people for God's own possession." This is true because they had been born again through the living and abiding word of God (1:23). Because of His ineffable love for sinners—even His enemies—God initiated redemption, sending His Son to be our Savior (Rom. 5, John 3:16). The Holy Spirit-inspired word of the gospel, as we received it by faith, became in us the Spirit-instilled seed of eternal life (I John 3:9). We who believe have been saved by a grace that is free, but certainly not cheap.

Peter said, we are the recipients of God's mercy, called from the darkness of unbelief and death into faith and light, and our redemption from bondage to sin and death was not with "perishable things like silver and gold . . . but with precious blood . . . the blood of Christ" (1 Pet. 1:18*ff*). We are born-again and blood-bought children of God, a tribute to His amazing love and grace. In God's estimation, we are worth the blood of His Son Jesus, the sinless sacrificial payment for our redemption.

Alexander Nisbet, seventeenth-century Scottish pastor, commenting on this passage, said we were purchased at "a dear rate."[2] While my wife and I visited Scotland, our hosts, realizing that we were on a budget, warned us that Edinburgh was "a dear city." "Dear" in that usage meant expensive. They also called us "Roger, dear" and "Nancy, dear." "Dear" means "expensive" and also "beloved." God shows us how dear we are to Him by paying the dearest rate for our salvation. How marvelous this is, especially in light of our former lostness, and helpless condition in which, as Paul said, we were "without hope and without God in the world" (Eph. 2:12).

But He has saved us, and He has called us to be His people. The biblical metaphor of the people of God as a building, a temple, is used and Peter said we as His people are building stones, having received our life and identity by coming to that Living Stone, that Rock of Ages, Jesus (1 Pet. 2:4-5).

By His grace, God has rescued us from the pits of death, and quarried us and gathered us to Himself. We now also are living stones. We share the nature of the Living Stone, Jesus, and He dwells in us through the Holy Spirit. We now have a personal relationship with Him, and keep on coming to Him in our relationship of trust and obedience. We are called to be His people, His children, loved, sought, reclaimed, and now been remade into His likeness.

To Accept His Place

Peter reminded us that God has called us not only to be His people, but to accept His unique place for us, which is His church. That church universal, the kingdom of God, finds expression in the functioning body, the local church, which is usually the idea intended by the New Testament word *ecclesia* which means "called ones" or those called out for a particular purpose. Though the temple building metaphor is used, the church clearly is the *people.*

I like the marquee in front of a church building in Nashville, Tennessee, which says "Woodmont Baptist Church gathers here," not "Woodmont Baptist Church." It designates the Woodmont Baptist Church only when they are "gathered" at that location. Apart from certain appointed times for meeting, that particular church is scattered throughout the city of Nashville.

Peter said, "coming to Him . . . you also, as living stones, are being built up as a spiritual house for a holy priesthood . . ." (v. 5).

The place of every child of God is in the temple, the church, the Body of Christ. The salvation experience is certainly individual, but not individualistic. Christ made the church as well as He made disciples. He made disciples to need the church, and the church to meet the needs of His people.

Paul, in Ephesians 2, described believers as building material that Christ gathers from oblivion and brings together to build into His temple (2:13), gathering from among the Jews, the religious, and the Gentiles, the pagans. People who once were hostile are brought near and placed into the same temple.

We have no jurisdiction over who joins the church. Whoever God saves and adds, we must accept—whatever their background. Regardless of who we are and how different we are, the stones all fit together in God's temple, because all are built and put together on the same foundation, Jesus Christ (Eph. 2:20; 1 Cor. 3:11). The Lord Jesus is the Foundation, the Corner, the Capstone, who holds us together with a common life, love, and purpose. We don't just tolerate, but we by grace and love, understand, and help one another.

Peter pulled together several Old Testament references to say we are God's people who have a place in the new temple—not the one made with hands—but saved and called together by grace. We *are* part of the temple, but also part of the new order of the priesthood. What a stupendous thought to these Jewish converts, from being nobodies to priests, a position previously held only by birthright!

In the Old Covenant order only those born in the Aaronic lineage could be priests, and only one could be High Priest and enter once a year into the Holy of Holies. But Peter reminded us that we in the church—all of the people of God—are now priests unto God, with constant access into His presence. We have a privileged relationship with God, but also a priestly responsibility to others.

We need each other! Only once does the singular word "saint" appear in the New Testament. Sixty-two times the plural is used, emphasizing the corporate nature of the Christian experience.[3] We need each other to fulfil our calling to be holy. What a humbling privilege and responsibility to be His people, and to be given a place in His temple and priesthood.

To Fulfil His Purpose

Peter, however, led us to consider the climactic thought: God's call to the Body of Christ is to fulfil His purpose in the world!

We have looked at the construction metaphor. God is building His church with living stones, not to create a comfortable sanctuary, but to make a useful, working, functional temple, with an active priesthood.

In the Old Testament, "churches," "called-out assemblies," were formed always for a purpose—to worship, to receive instruction, or to go out to battle, and to conquer. Here, Peter, quoting Old Testament passages, said we are "a chosen people, a royal priesthood, a holy nation, a people belonging to God, that you may declare the praises of him who called you out of darkness into his wonderful light" (1 Pet. 2:9). Here in a strong purpose clause (*"in order that"*), we are told that the church is *"to tell out,"* as His temple, as His priests, who God is and what He has done for us.

To fulfil that great purpose, we need more than balloons and records, even more than an imploring pastor and nominating committee. We need consecreated, purposeful priests, believers who accept their priestly calling. Our purpose as God's priests is that we tell out, show forth, and "advertise" the virtues of our God and of His gospel. We know His work, and we know what His gospel and grace have done for us. Our purpose is to make this known to others. Traditionally, for most Baptists, the priesthood of the believer has meant an individualistic approach to God. But that's only the first part. We have a duty, a purpose, a job to serve Him in His temple, through His church. We are to show forth the virtues of God.

If we are in touch with God, we will continue to abide in Him in holiness and obedience to His will. As we abide in Him, we take on a likeness to Him, and people will take notice that we have been with Jesus (Acts 4:13). No doubt as he was penning these words, Simon Peter remembered when he had made the great confession at Caesarea Philippi, when Jesus told him that he would be nick-named "Petros," (meaning "a smaller detachment of the massive ledge"⁴), and that upon the "Petra" (the Rock of Ages, the Foundation), He would build His church (Matt. 16:18).

God revealed Himself in His Son, the Living Stone, and now He makes Himself known through His witnesses, little stones, who bear a striking resemblance to Jesus, in our character and by our love for one another. "All men will know that you are my disciples if you love one another" (John 13:35). We reveal Him who is Perfect Love by this caring concern, this Godlike love.

We have already noted that the love that permeates all of holiness is love in the concrete, love that acts in behalf of others. As is impossible in another setting, love finds its deepest expressions in the life and ministries of a local church. Because of their commitment to Christ and the indwelling grace of God, members of the same local expression of the Body of Christ are able to cross all human and social barriers, reconcile all differences, and experience the genuine fellowship of the Holy Spirit.

This same love motivates the church in its mission to the world, which is the continuation of the mission of Jesus Christ, the Great Commission (Matt. 28:19-20; Acts 1:1,8). We fulfil the eternal purposes of Christ as we proclaim the gospel, make disciples, and seek to minister to the needs of individuals and influence the well-being of society. Because we are heirs and stewards of the completed work of Christ's atonement, and because He dwells in the totality of His Church through the Holy Spirit, we can now be a part of these "greater works" Jesus promised for us (John 14:12).

We are called to be a part of a great Kingdom endeavor—to follow the mandate of Christ in making disciples, extending the borders of the Kingdom until that day when Jesus comes again and all the kingdoms of the world become the Kingdom of our Lord and of His Christ (Rev. 11:15). Because the Kingdom is within the human heart, the primary task of the church is evangelizing the lost (Luke 17:21). To that end we must not only win the lost to faith, but disciple them in the faith, leading new converts to become holy and wholly obedient to Christ.

When, then, should we not only minister to the spiritual needs of the family of God, but also become a servant to the local and world community, representing Christ's loving, healing presence in the midst of a needy world? A holy church is necessarily a missionary church, realizing the purpose of God is to make known the holiness of His Name to all the ends of the earth (Ezek. 36:23; Zech. 14:20).

The purposes of a holy church will not be fulfilled without a holy and wholly committed people. The awesome task before the church will be energized, not by doing business as usual, but only as we seek the power of God that comes only to a holy, consecrated people. People and churches that have humbled themselves, prayed seeking the reviving face of God, and turned from their wicked ways, can expect God to hear from heaven, forgive their sins and heal their land (2 Chron. 7:14).

I ask you, in the march toward holiness, to join me in church, in remembering the church and your part in the church. We have a calling to be holy, but also to concern and involve ourselves in the evangelizing and encouragement of others who will hear the call.

Our motivation to remember the church and serve the church will not come with promotional gimmicks and the pleading of the pastor. Our motivation is the love and grace of God and the greatness and certainty of our calling and our task.

Howard Foshee told of a newspaper article he read concerning Dr. John Tyndall, the renowned British scientist who excelled in molecular physics. Someone asked Dr. Tyndall who had been the greatest influence upon his life. The great scientist answered quickly that the person of greatest influence had been an old friend who had lived with him through the years as a servant. Dr. Tyndall said, "Each morning my friend would knock on my bedroom door and call out: 'It is 7:00, sir. Get up! You have great work to do today!' "[5]

We also have great work to do. The march toward holiness leads us into the great work of the church. But we must continue to the end.

Notes

1. Lewis Drummond, *The Awakening that Must Come* (Nashville: Broadman Press, 1978), pp. 66-69.

2. Alexander Nisbet, *I & II Peter* (Edinburgh: The Banner of Truth Trust, 1982), p. 81.

3. David Watson, *Called and Committed: World-Changing Discipleship* (Wheaton, Ill.: Harold Shaw Publishers, 1982), p. 39.

4. A. T. Robertson, Vol. I, *Word Pictures in the New Testament* (Nashville: Sunday School Board of the SBC, 1930), p. 131.

5. Howard B. Foshee, *Now that You're a Deacon* (Nashville: Broadman Press, 1975), p. 9.

13

A Holy Church

And now, dear children, continue in him, so that when he appears we may be confident and unashamed before him at His coming. If you know that he is righteous, you know that everyone who does what is right has been born of him. How great is the love the Father has lavished on us, that we should be called children of God! And that is what we are! The reason the world does not know us is that it did not know him. Dear friends, now we are children of God, and what we will be has not yet been made known. But we know that when he appears, we shall be like him, for we shall see him as he is. Everyone who has this hope in him purifies himself, just as he is pure (1 John 2:28 to 3:3).

Most of life's vocations end in retirement, but our calling to holiness continues to the very end of mortal life itself. It was during their "post-retirement" years that both the apostles Paul and John addressed the need to continue in spiritual growth and in the development of holiness to the very end of our earthly pilgrimage. Paul expressed his intention to press on like an athlete toward the goal of winning the prize for faithfully running and completing the race of faith. As an aged apostle, Paul realized his need, along with all believers, to continue to grow in godliness and conformity to the character of Jesus Christ (Phil. 2:12-14).

In our text, 1 John 2:28 to 3:3, we noted that the dimension of hope is a tremendous incentive to our growth in holiness. Reminding us of our identity and privileges as God's children, the veteran apostle John put his exhortation in an eternal frame of reference. We are to be growing in holiness each day of our earthly pilgrimage, as we move along toward our final destiny of fully receiving the glorious inheritance of the children of God. Our progressive holiness is to continue to the end of our mortal lives, which shall give way to our immortal glory of absolute Christlikeness.

One of the most frequent problems I encounter in the counseling aspect of my pastoral ministry is low self-esteem, even on the part of longtime Christians. The irony of this problem is its existence, in epidemic proportions, during an era of unprecedented attempts to boost the human ego and sense of self-importance. The 70's was "the decade of the self," as the world promulgated theories like "do something for yourself," "take care of number one," and *I'm OK—You're OK*[1]

The people of the world, with self-help and the help of certain psychotherapists and pop psychologists tried to feel good about themselves, putting their desires before all other considerations. But strangely enough, in many cases these very people began to think not too highly, but too little of themselves. They have missed the most important consideration for their self-identity and self-worth, their relationship with God. They have never realized or have forgotten that they were created in God's image, that Christ died for them, and that they were meant for eternal, abundant life.

John wrote to remind believers of our tremendous worth in God's sight, and our glorious privileges and responsibility. But what he said, and what God says to us today in His Word, contains a crucial distinction from the self-esteem philosophies of the world. The world says we are to find a good feeling about ourselves by elevating our self-image and our self-opinion by our direct efforts and selfish pursuits. God's Word says, on the other hand, we are not to focus on what we think of ourselves, but rather on what God thinks of us. The Good News is that God thinks a lot more of us than we think of ourselves. If those of you who suffer from depression and poor self-image can come to grips with the message of this text, you will enter a bright new day of a perpetual and growing sense of self-worth as a child of God, as one of God's forever children.

Dignity

People of the world apart from Christ look for self-esteem by tracing their roots, hoping perhaps to find some signs of nobility in the family tree! Those who do not believe in the personal Creator, God, have to live with the alternate idea that their very existence is by chance evolution. The people of this world really don't understand who they are, and John says the world doesn't understand Christians (3:1). But, do we Christians understand who we are as people with divinely-bestowed dignity?

John rejoiced in the thought: "How great is the love the Father has lavished on us, that we should be called children of God! And that is what we are!"

We are His children because He loved us enough to send His Son to redeem us. The love of God is beyond anything on earth. It is heavenly, ineffable love. God loved us while we were His enemies enough to give His greatest gift. His grace provided for our eternal life, and by faith in Jesus we were born again, "born of Him" (2:29). We are born into the family of God, and as new creations if God we begin to take on a family resemblance to the Heavenly Father (2 Cor. 5:17). As His children, because of the prompting of the new indwelling Holy Spirit, we learn to call upon God in an intimate Father-child relationship (Rom. 8:15).

We come to Him boldly, with confidence, making our requests known and seeking His help, knowing that He who loved us as sinners certainly loves us in special ways as His children (Heb. 4:16). Because He has given us the greatest gift, He will give us whatever we need as His beloved children (Rom. 8:32). What dignity conferred upon us, as God's children! As we realize our privilege, we realize also a new power resident within us. John says we "know that he is righteous" (2:29). It's the intellectual certainty that God is perfectly sinless and absolutely loving. But now, because of our rebirth and remaking, we know by experience that we are His children because we are, for the first time, able to practice righteousness! We want to please, obey, and serve our Heavenly Father and have a power to break old habits and live a new kind of life, a godly life.

Charles Koller told a story that illustrates how the dignity of our self-identity determines our behavior.

> During slavery days, some Northern visitors in New Orleans were watching a company of slaves wearily shuffling along the dock, returning to their work. Spiritless, apparently indifferent to life itself, they were dragging themselves along. But one, in striking contrast, with head erect and with unbroken spirit, strode among them with the dignified bearing of a conqueror. "Who is that fellow?" someone asked. "Is he the straw boss; or the owner of the slaves?" "No," was the answer, "that fellow just can't get it out of his head that he is the son of a king."
>
> And so he was. He had been dragged into slavery as a small child, but had already been taught that he was no ordinary person; he was the son of a king, and must bear himself accordingly, as long as he lived. Now, after half a lifetime of hardship and abuse, which had broken the spirit of the others, he was still the son of a king! Such is the inspiration and the strength of the sons of God![2]

This child of an unknown king had a sense of dignity that transcended his circumstances and what others thought of him. If we just knew *whose* we are we would not have to worry about who we are. Because we are God's children, we know He has the highest ambition and aspirations for us. He does not want to deprive us of *one* thing that will add to our deepest joy. He has joys and blessings for us far higher than we have imagined, much less claimed for ourselves.

C. S. Lewis said,

Our Lord finds our desires, not too strong, but too weak. We are half-hearted creatures, fooling about with drink and sex and ambition when infinite joy is offered us, like an ignorant child who wants to go on making mud pies in a slum because he cannot imagine what is meant by the offer of a holiday at the sea. We are far too easily pleased.[3]

Destiny

Not all of life's vocations result in successful careers. Often, time runs out before an individual can reach his or her desired goals. Those outside of Christ who are trying desperately to improve their self-image and heighten their sense of self-worth by achieving certain goals are racing against time. Many are fearful that life's opportunities are passing them by. But John reminded us that for the child of God the best is yet to be. We have ever before us a glorious destiny beyond this world of time, space, and other limitations. The calling to holiness is a vocation with guaranteed success. Because God has purposed that we shall someday be conformed to the likeness of His Son we can rest assured that His will shall prevail (Rom. 8:29).

John cautioned against vain speculation, noting that only our experience of the hereafter will reveal the full extent of its blessings. Because this destiny is so far beyond the current level of our experience, the Bible describes heaven with symbols. We can be grateful for our limited comprehension of eternity because our limitation is a witness of its greatness. John stated simply the essense of our glorious destiny, that we shall be like Him. Let us be content to say with Richard Baxter:

> My knowledge of that life is small,
>   The eye of faith is dim;
> But tis enough that Christ knows all,
>   And I shall be like Him.[4]

The glory of God is His beauty, wealth, powers and all properties of His divine character. Man, in his sinful, fallen condition, cannot look upon the fullness of God's glory. Even Moses, the great man of God, was denied his request to look upon God's face, the fullness of His glory, being told that no one could look at God and live (Ex. 33:18ff). Even the child of God, who is now being gradually changed into Christ's likeness, cannot behold God's full glory because of the old sinful nature that remains. The full weight of glory we cannot bear, even as David could not wear Saul's armor (1 Sam. 17:39).

Yet, we someday shall behold our Savior, the now-glorified Son, whose appearance to Saul of Tarsus blinded his eyes. Jesus, the express image of the invisible God (Col. 1:15)—embodiment of all God is (Col. 1:19-20)—will receive us and encounter us face to face, and we shall then become like Him (1 John 3:2). Our eyes will not be blinded, but will with wonder and rapture, behold the fullness of His beauty and holiness, and thereupon we shall undergo a marvelous metamorphosis. We will then become all that God wanted us to be in the first place. The image of God will be fully restored, and not only will we be rid of sin's power, but the last vestige of our sinful nature will be banished and from that moment on we will be perfectly "conformed to the image of His Son" (Rom. 8:29).

We will receive our full inheritance as God's children, which is to be like Jesus. To be glorified is to share the holiness of Jesus, which includes both negative and positive holiness. We will be rid of sin's negative influence and its consequences, such as sickness, sadness, guilt, and death. But also we will have the powers of godliness; our glorified minds will comprehend the glories of God and His universe, and we will revel in the glories of His plans and purposes for the ages, which beforehand were hidden from us. We will have glorified bodies, like that of the resurrected Jesus, bodies recognizable but now unlimited by time, age, and space (Phil. 3:21).

All this will take place when we see Him, upon our passing

through death into Paradise (in which we will await the resurrection of the body at the return of Christ) or in our meeting Him upon His return to earth.

The child of God has an inestimable privilege right now, the dignity of belonging to God and assuming His likeness, experiencing His blessings, and moving toward the consummation of them all in eternity. What we are and have now is beyond comprehension, and how much more our destiny to become and to receive.

If we only knew these things, if we were more aware of our dignity and destiny, never would we fall into spiritual depression or ever doubt our worth and security as persons.

Duty

Social scientist, best-selling author, and pollster Daniel Yankelovich, has noted that "self-formers" who are living by their "new rules" of doing their own thing, in a desperate search for self-esteem and self-fulfillment are abandoning wholesale the old rules of commitment to relationships and traditional values.[5] For example, the housewife becomes fearful she is not experiencing life to the full, and she leaves her husband and maybe even her children on some romantic pursuit of her "true self." In doing so, she is betraying who she really is. Her commitments are part of her identity and her sense of duty is an important part of her sense of self-worth. The child of God has a strong sense of self-worth because of personal dignity and destiny, but also because of his or her duty to God.

John reminded his readers of the second coming of Christ, and warned them not to become speculative, but to be practical. Because Jesus is coming back, we must be about our duty, and must be busy—on the job—when He appears.

John said we are to abide in Him, which is to remain in close fellowship with our Lord. Jesus Himself describes this great responsibility and privilege as branches (believers) abiding in Him, the True Vine (John 15:1*ff*). The Christian life is primarily a relationship of faith, love, and fellowship. By the Holy Spirit, Jesus dwells in us and we are responsible to cultivate that relationship and friendship with Him (John 15:14). We, by growing communion, appropriate the fullness of His life imported through the Holy Spirit. As we abide, our joy increases as does our hope.

We are increasingly aware of our dignity and destiny, as we grow in hope. We learn to think in terms of eternity, and our values become fitting of pilgrims and sojourners. We lose our affection for temporal things and are not as devastated by misfortune. We start yearning for eternal rewards which culminate in the fulfillment of God's purpose for us, which is to be like Jesus. We Christians so need to break the spell of worldliness with its lie that this world is our home, that "all these other things" should consume our energies (see Matt. 6:33).

As we truly long to be as righteous as He is righteous, to be perfectly conformed to the image of Jesus, our longing will become our preparation. We will allow the Holy Spirit to transform our character into the likeness of Christ Himself (2 Cor. 3:18). As we long to see Jesus, we know the condition of seeing Him more clearly by faith right now is to become pure in heart (Matt. 5:8). We have the desire to experience the fullness of holiness which now we know only in part.

Without the holiness begun by the rebirth, we cannot hope for the perfect holiness in which we shall see the Lord (Heb. 12:14). Like the Israelites who were summoned to the theophany at Mt. Sinai, we also must consecrate ourselves now (Ex. 19:10*ff*). And, when we by faith see Him, we consequently become more like Him (2 Cor. 3:18). This process, called sanctification, will culminate when we see the glorified Jesus face to face (1 John 3:2).

Our duty is to abide in Jesus by obedience and ethical understanding, discipline, and growing purity. Jesus said as we abide in Him, the Word would make us clean and His pruning would make us more fruitful (John 15:1-2). God's truth, providence, and discipline transform our obedient, submissive lives. We cleanse ourselves from all defilements, "perfecting holiness in the fear of God" (2 Cor. 7:1).

A reverential fear of God is not a foreboding dread of God, but is rather a profound recognition of the right of a holy and loving God to demand our obedience in character and conduct. Though we are to enjoy the assurance of our final salvation, which is based upon our being put right with God by faith, we are nevertheless to live in the creative tension of anticipating the coming Day of the Lord. John admonished us to "continue in Him, so that when He appears we may be confident and unashamed before Him at His coming" (1 John 2:28).

We who are God's children also will face a judgment, but not to determine our eternal destiny, which is settled and secure. Rather, our judgment will reveal the quality of our service and the stewardship of our lives. Our eternal rewards will be based upon our faithfulness with the opportunities given to us (1 Cor. 3:10-15; Luke 19:11-27). Carelessness and unfaithfulness will give rise to uneasiness and shame at the unexpected return of Christ. Peter said the Day of the Lord will be a sudden and unexpected cataclysm of judgment:

> Since everything will be destroyed in this way, what kind of people ought you to be? You ought to live holy and godly lives as you look forward to the day of God and speed its coming (2 Pet. 3:11-12).

Our preparation for eternal glory is the fulfillment of our calling to be holy. Our goal is to "be blameless and holy in the presence of our God and Father when our Lord Jesus comes with all His holy ones" (1 Thess. 3:13). Although we know that heaven will be perfect bliss, untainted by any hint of wickedness or imperfection, yet Scripture teaches that degrees of eternal reward and blessedness will be determined by the degree of our diligence in our earthly march toward holiness.

The question asked by the writer of the Hebrews is searching indeed: "How shall we escape if we ignore such a great salvation?"

(Heb. 2:3). Our salvation was secured through the cross of our Lord Jesus Christ, and demands the response of our obedience. We are saved through the cross, but also the cross is the symbol and expression of our duty. We too must take up the cross of our self-denial and willingly share the mission, and even the sufferings, of our Lord before we may share in His eternal glory (John 16:20; Rom. 8:17). Through the eyes of faith we begin to see that "our light and momentary troubles are achieving for us an eternal glory that far outweighs them all" (2 Cor. 4:17). Our duty is to abide in the Christ of the cross.

When we share in His crucifixion, we who have died to the world no longer fear what the world can do to us or take from us. We are glory bound! Also, we pilgrims are of greater earthly good because we are heavenly minded. The greatest humanitarians of history have been those who served others because they realized the dignity and eternal destiny of every soul. Hear the testimony of Lord Shaftesbury, the great English social reformer near the end of his life: "I do not think that in the last forty years I have ever lived one conscious hour that was not influenced by the thought of our Lord's return."[6]

And, as God's forever children, we cannot think about our dignity and future destiny without thinking about and being deeply concerned about our neighbor's destiny. C. S. Lewis reminded us,

> It is a serious thing to live in a society of possible gods and goddesses to remember that the dullest and most uninteresting person you talk to may one day be a creature which, if you saw it now, you would be strongly tempted to worship, or else a horror and a corruption such as you now meet, if at all, only in a nightmare. All day long we are, in some degree, helping each other to one or other of these destinations. It is in the light of these overwhelming possibilities, it is with the awe and the circumspection proper to them, that we should conduct all our dealings with one another, all friendships, all loves, all play, all politics. There are no ordinary people.[7]

The spirit and character of holiness is deeply evangelical in nature. In the holiness and purity of heart that allows us to see God we grow in Christlike concern for the spiritual condition and destiny of others. We have a zeal and passion for their conversion to Christ, and yearn that on the day we receive the crown of life there will be with us many who will share eternity with us with whom we were privileged to share the message of salvation. Indeed, these converts, according to Paul, are part of our joy and our crown (Phil. 4:1). Evangelism is our duty and our privilege.

Colonel Clark, who for many years did evangelistic work in Chicago's Pacific Garden Mission, was asked why he worked day and night, sometimes to the point of exhaustion. He replied,

> "I think every night the last man will be saved at the mission and then Jesus will come. I want to be at my duty station when He comes."[8]

Our duty is to abide in Him and be diligent in the task Christ has given us. In the march toward holiness we must include this fourth step of continuing to the end and keeping our eye upon the End. The eternal perspective reminds us of the brevity of our earthly march, but also of the cruciality of each step in answering the call to be holy, a calling with eternal consequences.

Throughout the writing of this book I have been acutely aware of my audacity in even attempting to treat such a lofty and unfathomable subject. My attempt of this sacred subject reminds me of the temerarious and legendary author of the book, *Humility, and How I Achieved It!* Though mine has been a partial and inadequate treatment of the topic, I hope I have conveyed my role as a fellow pilgrim, seriously seeking to answer this unmistakable and unavoidable call to holiness. I want to be holy because God is holy. My prayer is that you join me in this aspiration of fulfillment expressed in God's Word.

May God himself, the God of peace, sanctify you through and

through. May your whole spirit, soul and body be kept blameless at the coming of our Lord Jesus Christ. The one who calls you is faithful and he will do it (1 Thess. 5:23-24).

Notes

1. Thomas A. Harris, *I'm O.K.—You're O.K.: A Practical Guide to Transactional Analysis* (New York: Harper & Row, 1967).

2. Charles W. Koller, *Expository Preaching without Notes* (Grand Rapids, Mich.: Baker Book House, 1962), p. 127.

3. C. S. Lewis, *The Weight of Glory and Other Addresses* (Grand Rapids, Mich.: Wm. B. Eerdmans, 1965), p. 2.

4. Quoted by Alexander Maclaren, *Expositions of Holy Scripture: First & Second Peter & First John* (Grand Rapids, Mich.: Baker Book House, 1974, reprinted), p. 309.

5. Daniel Yankelovich, New Rules: *Searching for Self-Fulfilment in a World Turned Upside Down* (New York: Bantom Books, 1982), pp. 1ff.

6. James Montgomery Boice, *The Last and the Future World* (Grand Rapids, Mich.: Zondervan Publishing House, 1974), p. 45.

7. C. S. Lewis, pp. 14-15.

8. W. Herschel Ford, *Simple Sermons about Jesus Christ* (Grand Rapids, Mich.: Zondervan Publishing House, 1961), p. 103.